The Letter
The Life of A Vietnam Tunnel Rat

By Joe "Louis" Loveless

Co-written by LaToya Loveless

Copyright © 2024 LaToya Loveless

All rights reserved.

Printed in the United States of America

Except as permitted under the U.S. Copyright Act of 1976, no part of this publication may be reproduced, distributed, transmitted in any form or by any means, stored in a database or retrieval system without the prior written permission of the publisher.

Table of Contents

Introduction

Chapter One - How It All Began

Chapter Two - The People in My Life

Chapter Three - Short Stories that Shaped Who I Am

Chapter Four - Getting Ready

Chapter Five - Vietnam

Chapter Six - Back Home

Chapter Seven - My Poetic Phase

Chapter Eight - Unexpected

Afterword

Message from son, Jarel Loveless

One of my first memories of my dad was when we ran across a man standing outside of his broken-down car. Even though it had been a long day, my dad stopped to help. We spent hours troubleshooting outside the automotive shop, until the man's car finally started. That's just the kind of man he was. He was incredibly selfless. I can't tell you how many times he was there for me when I needed him most. Even though he's not physically with us, his lessons live on through all of us who were lucky enough to know him.

Message from daughter, TaSharra Loveless-Dillard

"Call Joe" was the common phrase of my Dad's family and friends. He tinkered with many things, and everyone knew who to call when they needed help. If he didn't know how to fix something, he would find out and still help everyone. This book is dedicated to my Dad's drive to have always learned new things throughout his life. Now it is our job to keep not only his stories, but also those of other heroes going!

Introduction

If I had given up on life, no one would have cared. If I had resorted to a life of crime, no one would have blamed me; but I wanted to prove everyone wrong.

Regardless of the hand life deals you, it does not mean you have to follow it. Everyone faces hurdles and obstacles daily. I have been leaping over these hurdles all my life, barely getting over them. Occasionally, I tripped and fell, but I always got back up, brushed myself off, and continued to live.

There were many forks on my path of life that I could have chosen. A few times I am not proud of, but I knew I was the only one in control of my happiness, my decisions, and my destiny. I was compelled to write this book... let me rephrase that, I was spared to write this book.

Growing up, most of the little boys spent their time playing and enjoying the company of other little boys; there was nothing but fun and carefree days. Some of us were destined to have a difficult road to travel, and I was one of them.

I was so awed and intrigued with life that I began observing plants, animals, people, and anything that took a breath. I often laid in a field of sunflowers with my dog Bullet spending hours watching the butterflies and bees in flight navigating from flower to flower. As I stood eye level to the sunflowers, I sensed their urgency to live, waiting to be awakened by the soothing warmth of the next day's sun.

Some days I stared without blinking until tears flowed down my cheeks at the swollen belly tadpoles that swam in the shallow, stagnant water. I was hoping to see the miraculous moment they turned into frogs, but it never happened. That was life, carefree and peaceful. That was how it was meant to be, so I thought.

I never considered the hardships I endured throughout my life unique in any way because I went through extraordinary lengths to not write about them. Over the past thirty years, I held pen to paper waiting for inspiration to let the ink flow.

Could I have written *The Letter* book any sooner than now? More than likely not.

The catalyst, which guided me to write, occurred in 1971. I made a promise that if my life and soul were spared, I would write. Here we are thirty-four years later, and the words are just starting to flow; but then they stopped. I became overwhelmed with re-living my pain, so I began making excuses as to why I could not continue writing. I even tried to convince myself that the incidents in my life never happened.

For the last five years, the urge to write *The Letter* grew to the point where I could no longer resist. This book is a portal into my childhood and reliving the major stories in my life that prepared and helped me survive the Vietnam War.

I was really concerned about what people would say about me if they knew certain things. However, my life was spared just for the sole purpose of writing this book. Therefore, I knew I had to obey.

Some may not believe what I am about to write, and I respect your opinion. Nevertheless, *The Letter* has helped me to come to terms with myself for everything that has happened in my years of life on this Earth.

Revisiting my mental and emotional wounds is something I have avoided for many years. I know that each true-life story that I tell will be like a stitch being cut from my scarred wounds. I hope this book motivates you to keep pushing and trying when life throws you curve balls. If I survived my childhood and the emotional scars tied to Vietnam mental scars, then you too can survive anything in life.

Chapter One

How It All Began

My entire family moved to the thriving city of East St. Louis, Illinois because there was plenty of work. We lived in the South End in a city called Washington Park.

Growing up attending church on Sunday was a family tradition; it was the only day of the week to get with other family members, as well as playing with friends from the local church.

Every family worked all week long, either in the fields picking cotton or gathering food crops. We would put our best clothes on and would hold our Sunday shoes in our arms as we walked to church. Once there, we hid our old shoes in the weeds until we were ready to walk back home. After church all the family members gathered at one house to eat a large Sunday dinner. This was life!

We moved into a house that had a blackberry and two shade trees in the front yard. Being new to the area, I began thinking of ways to meet friends in the neighborhood.

On one sunny day I waited up in the blackberry tree for neighborhood kids to pass by so that I could entice them with berries. As I waited, hunger pains began twisting my stomach into knots, so I grabbed a handful of berries to silence my hunger. I then noticed a victim walking my way.

"These some good berries! You can have some." I said as I held out my hand to show him the big juicy berries.

The boy continued to walk, but he soon slowed down as he contemplated turning around.

"My name is Louis, what's yours?" I asked.

I purposely chewed loud on the berries smacking with my mouth open to entice him to stay and talk.

"Paul."

He then entered my yard, climbed up into the blackberry tree, and began eating the berries with me. He talked about how his mother and stepfather lived in the house next door to ours; but he, his brothers and sisters lived two houses further up.
Over time Paul became my best friend; but I never questioned why he did not live with his mother.

My neighborhood reflected a lot of the lifestyles of Southern cities where families migrated to. Everyone raised a garden either in their back yard or on a vacant plot of land close to their house.

The Mississippi Delta soil was called black gold in that era. As a small child, I believed this literally, so I spent many hours always digging trying to find the gold. The gardens planted in this soil flourished with the best tasting produce you could ever imagine, corn, tomatoes, okra, beans, watermelons, sweet potatoes, collards, turnips, and spinach greens. Everyone in the neighborhood also raised chickens and had eggs to share. We were a village.

I can remember being young moving into another but larger shotgun house, which was located right down the street. Unfortunately, this house, like others in the neighborhood, was not insulated. The rooms were in a straight line with no doors, therefore no privacy. During the winter, we used a wood-burning stove for heat. I remember during the cold mornings; Dad would call my brother to get out of bed to make a fire for the front room.

Even though I was son number two and younger, it seemed as if I was the one who made most of the fires. Often my brother would not respond when Dad called because he knew eventually, Dad would stop calling his name and start calling mine. Because we both slept in the same bed, I could see my brother laying there and laughing as he held the blanket over his mouth to keep from being heard.

"Joe Louis... Joe Louis... git' up and make a fir'!" my father yelled from his bed.

As soon as Dad called my name, I always jumped from the bed and proceeded to build the fire until the warmth from the stove raised the temperature in the front room. Afterwards, everyone else got up to start the day. The heat from the stove along with the morning words from Mom, and the occasional aroma of roasted peanuts baking made everything alright. I remember times when Mom would sometimes have company.

The elderly ladies would turn backwards to the stove and lift the back part of their skirt up to warm their butts while they talked. As a kid I thought that they were roasting their butts like the peanuts Mom put on the stove.

My Dad was a master at acquiring second-hand items from his many walking treks through the neighborhood. At times, it was embarrassing to see some of the items he would drag down the street for us to use. My father strategically placed large barrels around our house to catch the rainwater runoff, which we used to water the garden, wash our clothes, and feed the chickens because we did not have running water inside our house. Our water came from an underground stream that we tapped into via a pump. This water always had a strong iron taste that took our breath away. If we were thirsty, we had no choice but to drink it. When the water levels were not high enough to prime our pump, we had to rely on our neighbors for drinking water because they had indoor plumbing. As a child, I thought that they were rich.

We had a two-hole outhouse, and I was so proud. I would brag to the other boys about our outhouse until the day a lady visitor came in and sat right next to me. Too embarrassed to do or say anything, I just sat there waiting for her to leave. I never bragged about our outhouse ever again.

I was small in stature, so I had to do the dangerous tasks that my father and brother were too big to do. Our house, like many others in the neighborhood, did not have a foundation. It was built on strategically placed cinder blocks stacked too high ten feet apart. These blocks were not mortared so when they began to lean, it meant I was the one who crawled under the house to be the laborer for my dad who barked instructions.

On many occasions, I closed my eyes as I crawled on my stomach. The dirt was always wet, cold, and infested with crawling and digging bugs that ended up in the cuff-folds of my blue jeans. I never thought about the house collapsing on me because I was more concerned about the crawling things not the falling things.

I had a fear of heights and I believe my father knew I did. I believed that maybe going up the heights was one of my father's rituals to make me a man, but I just wanted to be a little boy. One time, I watched him as he built a makeshift ladder from pieces of discarded lumber. My stomach ached and was in knots because I knew that the ladder equaled heights and I was part of the equation.

"Dad, watcha' buildin'? "
"I need to fix a hole in this her' roof."

He tilted the ladder to lean on the side of the house. I turned and tried to walk away quietly without him noticing, but then I heard him say,

"Louis... help me."

I quickly spun around and grabbed the sides of the makeshift ladder with my dirty little hands,

"I'll hold the ladder for you Dad!"

I was trying to sound as young and innocent as possible to throw him off guard so that he would not send me up the ladder, but it didn't work. I hesitantly began climbing up like a scared cat.

"Don't look down!" he yelled up.

Easy for him to say, he's not the one on this ladder. I began thinking how many rungs are there on this ladder? Am I climbing to heaven? Will I fall? As I was standing on the last rung of the ladder, I did not know how to navigate onto the roof, but I did know if I slipped, I was looking at a sure death from falling. My mind began to wander even more.

"Crawl off the ladda' and git on the roof!" Dad yelled. As I reached the top of the ladder and the steeply angled roof, I prayed; Lord, if I slip and fall, please take me before I hit the ground.

"Dad, I can't stand up!" I yelled hoping to get sympathy.

My legs began feverishly shaking, I was scared to death. I could tell that his frustration with me was seeping through his words.

"You can!"
"No, I can't!"

My voice quivered from my fear of heights. I thought that if my life had to end, it would be from hunger not from stepping off the ladder, so I refused to stand up! I was determined and willing to remain where I was, in a crouched position until I died of starvation or thirst whichever came first. Dad knew I had drawn my line in the sand, so he instructed me to climb back down the ladder. Over the years, however, my fear of heights dissipated because it became a means for my future survival.

At the end of the street was a large bean field approximately a few miles long and at least one mile wide. Across the street was a vacant field, and behind our house was a set of train tracks.

One neighbor raised hogs and pigs in his backyard, and the other neighbor was an elderly lady whose front yard did not have a blade of grass or a pebble in it.

Her yard was always used for religious dances called, "The Rock" which was performed by female worshippers. I never understood what they were dancing for, but I knew it had to be for something important. As you can see, we had a plethora of events surrounding our shotgun house.

The Trains

During the day, I stood inside our fenced backyard mesmerized by the trains rolling back and forth as conductors switched from one set of tracks to the other. I grew to respect the power of the train and the finesse of the conductors.

"Hey Louis, I bet I can jump on the train, hold on with one hand and jump off while it's movin', but you can't!" Mike, one of the neighborhood boys said relishing in his belief that he could.

He taunted me as he had the biggest smirk on his face from ear to ear. My stomach churned because I was so nervous. I bawled my hand into a fist and shook it at him. I was so determined to prove him wrong, but I was secretly hoping my mother would appear on the back doorsteps to stop us, but she was nowhere in sight.

I was so petrified as I watched Mike run along the fast-moving train and then jump on with the grace of a cat, but deep down I knew I could not follow his lead. Mike eventually let go of the train railing and landed effortlessly back on his feet.

He then looked at me and began pointing and laughing hysterically because he could see the fear in my eyes. I stood there petrified because I did not want to go through with the dare, so Mike followed me back in the yard teasing and taunting me.

"You a scaredy cat Louis…scaredy cat…scaredy cat!"

I left Mike standing outside still laughing at me as I ran to the house to sulk and pout. That train caused me so much turmoil. In the beginning, I even had a problem sleeping because we were so close to the train tracks. As I laid in bed each night, the train's whistle blew at the highest ear-piercing tone constantly. I thought I was never going to sleep again.

At night I envisioned the train's conductor smirking as he blew the ear-piercing whistle.

I believed he took joy knowing that the shrill of the whistle awakened every man, woman, and child in the neighborhood.

I had nightmares of the train jumping the tracks, chasing me inside and outside our house, but over time, I became accustomed to and looked forward to the rhythmic melody of the train's wheels and whistle playing a soothing sonnet, which helped me sleep.

The Railroad Detectives

I loved playing in our yard, eating the berries with my friends, and watching the trains roll by. The gravel road that separated my back yard from the train tracks was used by railroad detectives who guarded the trains.

One night, as a group of us were walking, two detectives began driving up and down the road fast causing us to jump out of the way from being hit. They pulled next to us and one of the detectives leaned out the window and asked,

"Hey, you boys seen anyone break into any boxcars?"
"Nope."

The detectives stared at us for the longest, looking at our dirty blue jeans to see if we had any stolen items protruding from the top rim of our pockets. He spat his tobacco onto the ground in our direction and then they drove off.

After they drove away, we laughed amongst ourselves, we always said no because it was our way of getting back at them for making us jump out of the way. Overall, this was a nice neighborhood for us kids.

My Dad took care of the outside of the house and my mom took care of the inside, but this was how times were in the 40's and 50's.

Mom cooked our meals on the wood-burning stove in the kitchen which also doubled as our only source of heat on cold days and nights. A fire was made on one side and the other side was used for frying on top.

We also used an icebox to keep our food chilled, so every few days a block of ice had to be placed on top to keep it cool. Any remaining ice was put in a large hole in the backyard, lined with thick burlap material and layers of straw.

After placing the last lining of burlap and straw, we then covered it all with soil. It was a pain having to wait on the neighborhood iceman to deliver ice in his horse driven wagon.

One day Mom heard the trotting of the horse coming down the road,

"Joe Louis..." she yelled from the front room, *"go git' me two blocks of ice."*

I ran outside in my favorite cutoff blue jean shorts and t-shirt and waited for the iceman to pull up.

"Hey Mister...can we have two blocks of ice?"

He gently pulled the reins on his horse to stop. He then hopped off and walked to his wooden cart layered with straw without saying one word.

"Hey Mister, do you give your horse ice chips, he looks hot."

He still ignored me, as he lifted the ice up to begin chipping at it. Like ants, all the other kids from the neighborhood began to surround his wagon, waiting for the opportunity to catch an ice chip flying from his pick.

"You gonna give us a piece of ice?" I asked.

Sometimes he did, but most of the time he didn't. But that day was a rare time he decided to give us all ice chips. As I ate my ice chips after taking my mother her load, I pondered; could ice chips be savored, analyzed, and examined? What would happen if I swallowed whole ice chips? How long would it remain as ice in my stomach?

My friends and I sat in the dirt together as we slurped on the ice chips until it melted. Those were the days to savor!

The Runaway Truck

My family never owned a car, we walked wherever we needed to go, regardless of the distance. That was probably why I got motion sickness on those rare occasions when I had to ride a bus or a cab.

One of our neighbors owned a red truck that had brown wood panels around the open bed. He collected junk and allowed a few neighborhood boys to ride in the bed during his route. I wanted to ride in the bed with my friends, but my parents never let me.

I used to watch my friends vanish into the distance on those days and I fantasized that I was on the truck with them. I would close my eyes and picture me in the back with them laughing and joking around. I am free is what I wanted to shout at the top of my lungs.

But I was not free, reality beckoned me back. One day as I hid behind a tree, I watched my friends pile into the truck bed and shout with glee. As the truck began to move, I felt this was my only opportunity to escape reality, even though I knew the truck would be back shortly. If I did not seize this moment, I would never have the chance to ever ride.

I could no longer fight my desire to ride; so, with no hesitation, I darted from behind my hiding place and ran behind the truck. I ran as fast as my little legs would go, then my friends and family saw me and began yelling.

"Run Joe Louis, run! "cheered my friends as they piled to the back part of the truck.

"Joe Louis you betta' not! Git back here!" yelled my father at the top of his lungs as he hurriedly walked toward the truck.

Unfortunately, at that moment I could not distinguish what was being said or who was saying it. I was focused and determined to get on that truck.

The truck driver could not see me in his rear-view mirror; eventually I was able to catch up to the truck.

I managed to jump on the rear bumper, and I looked at my friends applauding me to make it. I wondered as the truck began to pick up speed.

Jubilance and exhilaration were quickly replaced with terror and fear as the speed started to take my breath away. The dust from the street swirled and encased me in a vortex of dirt. The truck became a beast in my mind, and I held on for dear life. It wanted to take my life!

I was no longer able to hear or see my friends in the back of the truck because of the dirt; I was truly on my own. My hands trembled and ached as the beast tried to fling me from its body.

"How dare you climb onto me without my permission...get off!" I imagined the truck angrily yelling.

My arms cried out in pain from desperately holding on as the feeling of my flesh being ripped from my body became evident. My thoughts began to wander...the beast took my breath, now it wanted to take my body!

Even though the truck drove faster and faster, it seemed everything was in slow motion. My mind was telling me not to let go, but I could no longer resist and so I did it; I let go.

The speed of the truck caused my body to spin in midair and I didn't stop until my head faced the dirt road and I hit the ground. I was upside down sliding as dirt flew in the air. I don't know how far I traveled because all I could think about was the spanking, I was going to get for jumping on the truck.

The commotion of all the people got the truck driver's attention, so he stopped. I remember watching everyone run towards me from all different directions. I was sure my dad was furious, but to my surprise he did not spank me. I believe he was more thankful that I was alive and that I did not break my neck or any other body part.

As I laid in the street no one said a word. They all hovered over me gasping and waiting for me to make a move. I slowly lifted my head then the rest of my body. As I stood to my feet, my dad dusted my jeans off from all the dirt compounded on them. I was then led home by his strong arm, that was my first and last ride on the red truck.

The Tree House

When I became an adult, I pondered about the games we played as children and wondered how we survived. We did not realize how dangerous these games were, but looking back they were our rite of passage into manhood.

None of us had any idea what life was about, and how our friendship and life obstacles were preparing us for the world beyond our neighborhood. We were in the process of learning how to survive in the harsh environment we grew up in.

Every Summer morning, when I heard the neighborhood dogs barking, I knew that meant Bobby, who lived five houses down, was outside. He was always the first up, so he waited for the rest of us to wake up and come outside. As always, I rushed to put my clothes on to get outside and climb the tree with him.

"What we doin' today?" I asked as I reached for the next tree branch to climb higher.

We sat on the thickest branch planning the day's adventure as dogs sat underneath the tree. We always played outside if the weather was nice.

One fun game we loved to play during the hot and dry days of Summer was filling old car tires with dry soil, and then rolling them down the street making clouds of dust. Bobby was the master at making the most dust fly from his tire.

He purposely waited for the girls in the neighborhood to start jumping rope and then he raced by them with dust billowing behind him. That was so much fun!

On rainy days, we watched our favorite television show, Tarzan. We wanted to be just like him, so we built a treehouse in an abandoned field that had tall trees growing like the ones we saw on television. We scavenged for old boards, doors, and any other building material we could use to build our tree house.

First, we scouted for a tree that had the perfect branches and we weren't concerned that the branches were high above the ground because we were fearless! Getting hurt was the furthest thing from our minds.

Working from sunup to sundown on our tree house was all we cared about. Our parents would not have approved of us being so high, so we didn't tell them. Finally done with building the unstable, wobbly, and rickety tree house, we were able spend hours and hours inside.

To finish it off, we added a "No Girls Allowed" sign on the outside door.

One day as we sat inside laughing and talking, dark puffy clouds quickly formed and rolled over the field, but we did not want to go home and end our fun, so we waited until it began raining.

As we huddled in our small tree house, the clouds grew even bigger. They looked like balls of cotton dipped in black ink and were beautiful yet ominous simultaneously.

We were committed to remain in the tree house until the storm passed, but the rain dropped harder and harder, as the tree began to sway more and more violently. We joked but nervously laughed about possibly having to abandon ship and having to run home in the hard pellet raindrops.

Without warning, the tree house started leaning and then coming apart piece by piece. As my friends scurried to get out, I told them I would be the captain of the ship and ensure everyone was safely out before climbing down.

Just as the last boy's foot touched the ground, the tree house and I started falling to the ground. Amid my falling, everything seemed to move in slow motion. I was frantically flailing my arms side to side and kicking until a big thud on the ground was heard. The tree house landed on one side and I on the other.

I did not know which hurt worse, my scrapes and bruises or the rain pummeling me on my face. After catching my breath, I was able to stand so I knew I was okay.

All of us started running, the thought of dying from the high tree house never crossed our mind.

We were disheartened because all the hard work we put into building our tree house was now lost forever.

Escapades

Tarzan was a free spirit, an outstanding swimmer, and loved being outdoors like us. During rain downpours, we would go outside to get drenched and pretend to swim like Tarzan.

Whenever it rained for long periods of time, there was a field that transformed into a small lake because the majority of rain runoff from surrounding streets flowed and collected there. The small lake came alive with wildlife: frogs, rabbits, birds, an occasional beaver, and all types of vegetation.

This temporary lake was deep enough to drown all of us and none of us knew how to swim. So instead of trying to swim we thought about making a raft for the temporary lake. Whatever material we could find is what we used to build our raft from scratch.

After building the raft, all of us immediately piled in the raft and paddled to the middle of the lake, which was fifty yards from land. Once we floated to the middle of the lake, the raft began to break apart. We tried to paddle back to shore as fast as our makeshift paddles would move us, but we were losing pieces of the raft rapidly and sinking. We all thought we would drown before reaching the land.

I extended the paddle deep into the water thinking this would move the raft faster, but it didn't. As I peered in the water looking at my reflection, I pondered what to do if the raft gives out. We thought we were going to drown but no one wanted to cry out.

Working as a team, we eventually made it back to land and jumped off.

We let the remaining pieces float back into the water to sink. That was our last escapade of building our own raft. How could we? This one almost took our life!

Unlike rafts, we thought we were good at building teepees or so we thought. We built them with the reeds, prairie grass and different plants which grew in the field. We even stripped the bark from trees and used it as rope. Once again from sunup to sundown we built our teepee, then afterwards we sat inside eating and laying in it for hours until it was time to go home.

One morning, I got up early and ran to where we had built our teepee. I could not wait until the other boys arrived. I decided to wait inside so I removed the straw from the entrance and went in. The straw was comfortable and warm as I laid down. I enjoyed being in the teepee alone, but I soon began feeling a concentrated warmth close to my right jaw.

Not knowing what it was, I slowly turned my head, to see a set of snake eyes staring back at me. Paralyzed with fear and being afraid I could not yell.

If I did, I thought the snake would jump and slither into my mouth, but if I laid extremely still and waited for the other boys then they would help me. I had no idea if the snake was poisonous or if the venom would kill me before I made it home.

It was an eternity laying there with the snake hissing and staring; I could not stand it any longer. I decided I was going to jump up and run but I knew if I rolled away slowly, the snake would coil, strike, and bite me.

So, I decided to spring straight up fast like a cat which would cause the snake to be startled and slither away in the opposite direction. I concentrated on having all my strength ready in my legs and arms.

After counting backwards from three, I sprang straight up through the top of the teepee closing my eyes because I did not want to see the snake springing to bite me. Once I stood up, I thought the snake was hanging on to me, so I jumped around even more patting myself all over. Luckily, the snake was not on me, nor did I get bitten. I rushed and ran back home to wait for my friends so that I could tell them all about my escapade.

One evening as we walked along the train tracks returning home from one of our excursions, we discovered a hidden camp used by traveling hobos. The camp was hidden among the tall weeds adjacent to the train tracks, so we named this place Hobo Jungle. The weeds and underbrush in the jungle were so thick, not even the railroad detectives knew the jungle existed, especially during the Summer.

The traveling hobos rode the trains in and out of town looking for work and they used the camp to eat and sleep. They had their own understanding to not pilfer through each other's possessions that were left behind.

When they were not there, my friends and I pretended to be the hobos and we spent hours lurking around in their jungle as we ate their food since we rarely saw them.

Later in life, I often wondered what would have happened to us if we were caught or hurt by the hobos in the jungle. Our parents would not have known where to start searching for us if we were kidnapped, but luckily none of us succumbed to that fate.

Fearless

Looking back, we were fearless! We did not think about getting hurt with any of the escapades we ventured on, but there was one time that we really tested the envelope.

Building tunnels became an active addition to being one of our adventures, which we did every Summer in an open field. The first year, the tunnels weren't too badly built, but the second year is when we really got in trouble because we dug them deeper than before.

We did not know anything about tunnels potentially collapsing because we were kids. Our first set of tunnels were a few feet straight into a clay hill, but that was not daring enough for us, so we decided to dig the tunnels down four to five feet then at an angle to make it about ten feet.

When we had turf wars with boys who lived on the other side of the highway, these tunnels came in handy. We hid in them and waited for our prey to enter the open field.

Once our lookout gave the signal, we popped out the tunnels as if we had springs on our feet.

We threw concrete rocks and shot handmade spears at them sending them yelling and screaming back across the highway. Looking back, it's amazing that we did not seriously hurt anyone.

We dug another hole a few feet down on their side of the highway, put sharpened sticks in it then covered the hole with reeds and straw. We never knew if someone fell inside and got hurt. As I said before, we were a daring bunch of boys.

A lot of the tunnels we dug only had one way in and one way out. Sometimes we would go down in one of the tunnels and wait until the other boys filled the opening with straw and then ignited it. The purpose was to see how long each of us could endure the smoke within the tunnel.

It was my turn in the tunnel, and I chose the one that had two openings because if the fire got too large or the smoke became unbearable; I could crawl out the other side. This tunnel had a 4 ft tee right in the center of both exits.

I crawled inside and waited for my friends to ignite the straw, except my friends did the unthinkable. It wasn't long before I started hearing the crackling of fire at both ends of the tunnel. The tunnel was immediately filled with a cloud of thick white smoke, and I was trapped.

I crawled to the tee part of the tunnel, wrapped my shirt around my face and took slow breaths to preserve the good air. I do not know how long the fire burned, but eventually it burned itself out. As I crawled through the embers, the smell was stifling. I never wanted to go inside another tunnel again, but little did I know that I would in the future, and it would be home.

During the fall of each year, we knew a farmer that lived ten miles away and it was time to prep his corn and wheat fields for harvest. We always played a game once a year that we called Run and Duck. All the boys who wanted to play met in the field early in the morning to begin our long walk to the farmer's field.

We carried salt wrapped in paper for the gardens we stopped at along the way. We ate fresh tomatoes, cucumbers, and ears of corn.

As we approached the farmer's field, we made sure he was outside. Crouching down and crawling we proceeded to get as close as possible without him seeing us as he continued to sway in his rocking chair on his front porch.

When we believed that we were close enough we jumped up and yelled right in front of him.

As we turned and began running back through his field, we knew that he would fumble with his rifle first. We were too fast for him to catch us, however, that didn't stop the many bullets whizzing by our heads as we ran away. I do not know if the farmer was trying to hit us or if he was trying to frighten us. We walked back home laughing and patting each other on the back reliving the moment.

Stealing Puppies

We loved all animals, except cats because they did not protect or hunt; plus, they were just weird. Like ants, we occasionally got the urge to invade surrounding neighborhoods that looked abandoned.

One day, we passed an old, dilapidated house. We became quiet and stood motionless, straining to hear the strange sounds that were coming from the house. We deciphered that the sounds were the whimpering and yelping of newborn puppies.

We followed the sounds to the back porch. We crouched down on the porch and looked through the gaps in the boards to see a litter of puppies and we had to get them.

The porch was too low for us to crawl under, so to extract them, we decided to run home and get tools to pry the boards from the porch. When we returned to the house, we started to bang, pound, and pull on the boards. After removing at least three boards, we stopped to rest because it was exhausting work. We didn't think anyone lived in the house, because they never came out despite all the noise that we were making.

After removing a couple more boards, the opening became wide enough to step down into the hole since I was the smallest. I crouched down not to hit my head on the top of the porch, then began carefully lifting the puppies out one by one.

As I handed the newborn puppies to my friends who eagerly waited to hold them, there was a creaking noise that made my friends turn around to look. The back door opened slowly like a scene from a horror movie.

Time seemingly stopped for us, and we all froze in our tracks. After the elderly lady stepped out, she kneeled to look under the porch. She pointed the biggest shotgun I had ever seen, directly at my face. Looking down at the barrel of the shotgun, I was so petrified that I could not make a sound. Her hand shook feverishly as she tried to point the gun and asked,

"Whatcha' doin' unda my porch?"

"We-we just wanted the puppies." I stuttered.

"Put 'em back and GIT!" she demanded.

One by one, my friends quickly handed the puppies to me as I put them back on their makeshift dirt bed under the porch. I then crawled from under her porch and fixed my eyes back on the rifle that was pointed at us.

We slowly walked backwards out of her yard, yet still fearful that she would get the courage to shoot. Once we got a few yards from her house, we turned around and ran as fast as we could. I kept waiting for the bullet from her pistol to enter my back, but she never fired.

Once we made it to my house, we sat around and joked about how scared we were, then we talked about what we were going to do the next day.

Chapter Two

The People in My Life

My Father

My father spent most of his available time working on the neighborhood church, even though our own house needed major repairs. We had window frames that needed to be painted, screens that needed to be replaced and holes in the roof that needed patching.

Attending church on Sunday was a part of everyone's life and my father was one of the Deacons. My brother, sisters, and I had a Saturday night ritual of getting him ready for evening church service.

My brother and I were responsible for cleaning and shining his shoes and my sisters were responsible for fixing his hair. As I laid on the floor watching them get him ready, I wondered why his hair was jet black, long, and curly but mine was short and nappy. I did not know at the time that he was part Indian.

My father looked so impressive in his white jacket, gloves, shiny shoes and long, curly black hair. When he was clean like this, I wanted everyone to know he was my father, but unfortunately, that was only twice a week.

He was cold at times because he treated me differently than my other siblings. I wondered if it was because my skin was darker and that I did not look like the rest of them.

There were times when he was gentle as a lamb and strong as an ox; I never heard him use profanity or a negative word against anyone. The first few years of my life, everything I did was to gain his approval. I believed and could see that my father loved my sisters; but for my brother and I, he would not say or show it.

My father grew up in an era where it was believed that boys should not show affection. Unfortunately, I learned this from him as I grew up. I remember playing as a child then falling scraping my knee and elbow to the bone. I did not cry out or shed a tear because I believed my father would be ashamed of me.

He was not a disciplinarian; I can count on one hand the number of times he punished me, even though I deserved it because me and my friends were very mischievous.

When I was eight years old, I took a stand. I knew it would be my last whipping from my father. All of us had to take regularly scheduled tablespoons of Castor Oil. Not only did it smell horrific, but it was thick and slid slowly down your throat.

I decided, on that day, enough was enough! I would never take another tablespoon of Castor Oil ever again. As I waited in line behind my sisters and brother, I looked at the newspaper, which covered the window in the kitchen and I burned the date into my mind, September ninth.

I stood in front of my father scared, but defiant as he poured the slimy Castor Oil onto the Army tablespoon. I watched as the thick liquid oozed from the bottle. The thought of swallowing the Castor Oil made me gag before he even told me to open my mouth.

My father lowered the spoon down and held it in front of my lips, waiting for me to open wide. I stood there, arms crossed and a frown on my face. I was not going to part my lips. This was the first and only time I refused to obey my father.

"Open yer' mouth." Dad said holding the spoon to my lips.

Refusing to open my mouth, my legs trembled as I stood there and before I knew it, he reached to take his belt off.

I thought my father was going to either kill me or I was going to drop dead because of fear.

"Joe Louis you gonna git' a whooping or are you gonna open yer' mouth to take this medicine?"

Dad yelled while the spoon was suspended in mid-air shook from the vibration in his voice.

I shook my nappy head no as a defiant gesture that I was sticking to my principles. As he slowly raised his belt, I grimaced and tensed the left side of my body to receive the hit. Down came the belt against my leg, but I felt no pain from the impact.

I was committed to my decision, and I stood there more determined than ever not to open my mouth or shed a tear, he will have to kill me. As my father looked down into my water filled eyes, it was at that moment he realized that I was his son; tough as nails and willing to die for personal principles.

"Git' outside and play!"

Without saying a word, I ran as fast as my ashy legs would carry me and I never took Caster Oil again.

My father worked as a laborer in a warehouse to support our family. Some evenings he returned home covered by the smell of different chemicals. We did not own a car, so he would leave for work early each morning walking and returning home at different hours, based on what he had to do that day.

He walked in rain, snow, sleet, and whatever other elements nature threw at him. Sometimes, I got up with Dad to walk with him down the tracks. He sometimes would give me a piece of his sweet bread or his sandwich. Now looking back, I believe this was his way of showing me love.

One Friday, Dad did not return home at his normal time. I remember my mother getting all of us kids together and we followed behind her down the same path Dad takes each morning. We eventually found him unconscious under a bridge.

Someone tried to rob him because his check was torn up and scattered around his body. As I picked up the pieces of his check, I read the total amount, $125.00. At the time I thought that was a lot of money. He managed to get up and walk back home with us.

My father always had lofty, outlandish ideas. The few times he and I sat down to talk, I saw him through a different set of eyes.

He wanted to build a store in our backyard, so he supervised the construction as Sammy and I were the laborers. I was so excited and could not wait until it was completed. As I handed dad one board after another to cut and nail to the side of the building, I daydreamed about all the money we would make.

A month passed and everything was complete. The only thing left was to buy the cookies and candy for the stores grand opening, but Sammy and I were not allowed to taste test anything.

One day me and Sammy were outside sitting on the porch,

"I want some of that candy!" Sammy said as he threw a rock on the ground.

He was adamant that he was going to get some candy. He was three years older than me, so I believed he always knew what was best.

"But how we gonna git the cookies Sam?"
"We gonna wait 'til dark and go in the roof."

We knew what we were about to do was wrong, but we wanted those cookies. When night came, me and Sammy put on black masks that we made from spare pieces of cloth found in mom's sewing basket. We did this because on television we knew that good guys wore white, and the bad guys wore black. So, we waited until everyone was asleep and then we sneaked outside.

"Hey Sam, how we gonna get up there?"
"Let's get the ladder so we can go up."

We grabbed the ladder and carefully leaned it against the building.

"You go up first," Sammy said as he held on to the bottom half of the ladder.

I wanted to chicken out, rip the villain mask off my face and run screaming to Mom, but I took the first step up the ladder. My hand touched one of the pieces of board, and I immediately pulled it back,

>"Ouch! I got a splinter in my hand!"

>"Shhh... shut up... you gonna wake mom and dad up!"

Even though I was convinced this was God's way of saying that we should not be doing this, I continued to climb. I took another step up the ladder one at a time until I made it to the top waiting for Sammy.
Slowly and carefully, we walked across the roof over to the hole We held on to the broken pieces of wood as we climbed down then jumped onto the top of the tall wooden display shelf.
Once inside, we opened the doors of the wooden case where all the cookies and candy were stored and proceeded to eat until we couldn't eat anymore. As I sat on the floor, with candy and cookie wrapping paper all around me and my stomach bloated, I looked at my brother,

>"I'm full Sam,"

We were so bloated, and chocolate was all around our lips.

>"Sam, how we gonna get out?"

We didn't think of an exit strategy, and we were too short to climb back up the wooden cabinet, so we just opened the front door and tiptoed back into the house. Later that night, my brother and I had stomach aches so bad that mom had to give us medicine. We moaned and groaned all night long from all the sweet chocolate. That was our punishment, a night of misery.

Mom leaned down to rub my stomach,

"Mom, we went in the store and ate all the cookies and candy."

I tearfully confessed because I felt so guilty with her taking care of us. Dad never spoke a word about what we did.

In addition to the store, Dad began building a theater for us in the back yard in front of the chicken coop. This was the only dream he talked about with so much excitement. As usual, my brother and I were his laborers, and slowly the theater took shape.

I tried not to get excited about the theater because I did not want my hopes to be crushed. Before the roof was added, we started to put benches inside which he salvaged from a demolition project.

Then for reason the project stalled. Sometimes I sat in the theater alone and thought about how it would look once it was completed, but soon the theater became scrap just like the candy store.

One evening I peered through the back window and saw my father walking with a hammer in his hand, he began to demolish the theater walls.

He was quiet and looked disappointed; he did not even ask for help. I ran outside, picked up another hammer and helped him knock the planks from the side of the theater. I didn't ask why he was tearing it down, we just continued to work in silence until the job was done. He was always a dreamer.

My Mother

As a kid, I felt that my Haitian mother was a saint, because she never had a bad word to say against anyone, not even about my father. Growing up I was so close to my mother, because she was the only person, I shared my deepest thoughts and dreams with.

Before I realized how poor we were, I remember mom saying she was never hungry when it came time for her to divide sweets among us kids.

Back then females who came from the North brought clay dirt with them when they visited their family in the South. I didn't know if that was abnormal or if it was a tradition in the family. I watched in amazement as mom would put a small portion of the clay dirt on top of our wood stove.

She watched with anticipation until it dried. Once done, Mom would break the clay dirt and then chew it as if she was eating the finest cut of meat.

"Can I have a piece?" I asked as I twisted side to side while leaning on her leg looking as innocent as I could.

But she always said no. When the clay dirt supply ran out, the females replaced it with Argo starch because it had the same consistency. The Argo starch held females over until another shipment of clay dirt was delivered.

I remember how my mother used her bare hands and a washboard to wash our clothes. One day, I watched her use the board and wondered what was so difficult about washing clothes on it.

So, when she walked away, I rushed over. As I peered around the corner looking back to make sure I didn't get caught, I dunked my hand in the tub to pull an item of clothing out. I then started to rub the shirt up and down over the scales on the board. As I lifted the shirt a second time, I did not notice that there was nothing between my knuckle and the washboard, and in one quick movement the skin from my knuckle peeled off.

I jerked back and ran from the room flinging my hand side to side in pain. I wanted to scream out loud and run to my mother to tell her about my injury, but I couldn't because I wasn't supposed to be messing with the washboard in the first place. I thought it wasn't fair. I had an injury, and I couldn't go to my mother for consolation.

A few years had passed, and we finally were able to get a washing machine that Dad drug home after one of his excursions. We got a washing machine that had two wringers which pressed the water from the clothes with an on/off switch. After the clothes swished around the machine for a while, we had to manually feed the clothes through these wringers.

My sister was feeding the clothes through one of the wringers and somehow it grabbed her arm and pulled it through up to her elbow.

When her arm could go no further, the wringer continued to spin which caused a nasty burn on her arm. She started screaming so loud that my mother rushed in, hit the wringer release lever, and pulled her arm out. After seeing how much pain my sister was in and the bruise that it caused, I never wanted to feed the clothes.

There was a moment when my mother didn't live with us. I remember sitting in Mom's room watching her and my newborn sister laying in the bed, and I saw how sad her eyes looked.

I ran outside and began digging in my lucky hiding spot, flinging dirt everywhere rushing to get back to my mother's bedside. The dirt covered my pants and shirt, but I wanted to retrieve my most prized possessions: a shiny rock, a cat eye marble, and a stained popsicle stick which I kept in a shoebox.

Surely, mom could not remain sad with these treasures in her hands, or so I thought. She eventually left anyway. As a child I struggled with her leaving my dad, brother, and sisters, but most of all I struggled that she left me.

I saw my mother and father fight only one time. I knew she was angry because she had made a fist, but Dad held her arms, and pushed her backwards where she hit the wall. I still see him pushing her to this day and the sadness in her eyes.

I wanted to hit him for pushing my mom, but I was small and all I could do was watch. I felt so bad because I believed that a little boy should always protect his mother.

I know my mother did not want to leave us behind, but I knew she felt as if she had no choice. Her heart ached as she walked out the back door to start the trek to her sister's house. That evening, I waited for her, but she did not come home.

A few days had passed, my father dressed us in our Sunday clothes to walk to my aunt's house. I didn't want to walk; I wanted to run to my mother. I wondered if she missed me and if she still remembered how I looked.

As we got to the corner of the street, my father stopped us and gave us a scripted speech to say.

    "Tell yer' mom you wan' her home...say you hungre and hav' no food."

I was confused because I was thinking that a mother knows how her children feel regardless of the words they say. We all did as Dad had instructed us to do, but Mom still resisted all efforts to move back home. The men in my family showed little to no emotion, let alone cry, so I tried as hard as I could to be a man.

    It was a somber visit, and I felt that mom was not coming back with us that night. I bit my lip to fight back the tears as my brother, sisters, and I waved goodbye to her as she stood outside and watched until we turned the corner heading back home.

    A few more days passed, before my father decided to move us closer into another small shotgun house one street over from where she was staying. Dad packed all our belongings and moved us so fast that I did not have time to say goodbye to my friends, but I didn't care because I wanted to be around my mother. In less than a month, mom finally moved back in with us, and I was happy once again.

    Growing up, my mother rarely left the house, but I didn't understand why. When I became an adult, I wanted to find out why she acted differently than the other mothers in the neighborhood. I did some research and determined she suffered from agoraphobia, the fear of being in open spaces.

    That explains why my mother always ordered our clothes and shoes from catalogues, because of her fear. I wondered if the people in the warehouse thought it was strange to receive a request in the mail to send a pair of shoes the same length of the string she left in the envelope.

    We also had specific days of the week where we had to stay home, Monday was my assigned day. When she mustered up the courage to go to a store, one of us had to stand behind her while the other stood in front. She did not want anyone standing behind her in line or getting too close to her. But through it all, I loved my mother.

Brothers and Sisters

Looking back on the relationships with each brother and sister, I always wondered why I felt dramatically different, and how it evolved to be that way.

My older sister tried to function as our mother when we had to take care of ourselves. She tried to emulate the things Mom did, but she did not have all the pieces to replicate her. I'll never forget when she tried to cook mom's cornbread; I had no choice but to eat the mysterious product she created because I didn't want to be hungry that night…so I tried to eat it.

My older brother was named after my father. More times than I want to admit, he tried to act as if he was our father. We did not bond the way I thought brothers should bond so growing up I only went to him when I needed some muscle against someone.

My third sister and I had a special bond because we took care of each other to ensure we both survived. She was my protector even took over a couple of fist fights for me and won.

The fifth sister was a tomboy; I took her with me to play as many boy games as I could. She was never a prissy girl; she was hard and resilient.

When I was a kid, I knew that every time mom's stomach was fat, it was time for another kid to be born. I used to celebrate by eating a Big-Time candy bar between two saltine crackers.

We were all born at home except for one of my sisters so when it was time for mom to deliver, a bed sheet was draped across the doorway of our shotgun house. A strange lady always showed up to everyone's house that had the bed sheet draped on the doorway.

This lady came into our house, shuffled into the room Mom was in stayed a few minutes then left. Mom always had a baby laying in her arms as she laid in the bed, but I never heard any of them yelling or screaming. I rarely held or played with any of them because I felt that my responsibility was to make sure that the baby was always safe when I was around.

Me

And then there's me. Once I grew older, I found out that all the babies in my neighborhood born at home were delivered by the same old lady. She charged $50 dollars, but back in those times $50 was equivalent to $50 thousand dollars because everyone was poor.

Since my mother and father did not have the $50.00 immediately, they paid a little at a time. Whenever the lady came to our house to collect money, I always hid from her because I thought she was a witch waiting to take little kids when their parents weren't looking.

She scared me because every time she saw me, she would point her crooked finger, leaned down to my level and say,

"You not paid fo' so you mine, I'mma take you to help dulivr' shildrn'!"

She barely had any teeth so some words she couldn't say and she always had a ripe smell to her.

"Don't let her take me! I don't wanna deliver babies!"

I did not want this woman to take me, so I wrapped my arms around my mother's leg and held on for dear life.

This woman looked 200-years old and was big and round. I kept a diligent eye opened for the witch every day; always looking up the street to catch a glimpse of her before she caught one of me.

Then one day I spotted her so I took off running towards my mother.

"Mom, she comin'! She comin' down the street!"

I was determined to find a hiding place. The witch leaned on her crooked wooden cane as she walked while kicking dirt from the front of her shoes. She wore her tattered, dirty, and dried blood-stained apron with large pockets.

After every few steps, she paused and lifted her head sniffing the air trying to smell any pending births. I wondered what she was carrying in the huge pockets on that apron; maybe she was carrying the little babies whose mom and dad could not pay for them.

My heart was pounding, as I watched from my hiding spot her entering our house and looking around. I believed she was looking for a kid to devour or for one to deliver. Mom welcomed her in and placed money into her outreached hand from a milk carton. The witch then turned and shuffled back out the door, but I waited until she was a safe distance down the road before I came out of my hiding place.

"Mom, I don't want her comin' 'round here, she may put me in her apron, and you would never see me again."

I was not old enough to attend school but, my brother and two older sisters were. They would begin to get ready for school after my father left for work. Every morning, after closing the front door I sat on the front porch waiting for their lunch break.

Our front porch was enclosed with a screen, so I had a little protection from the weather elements. Since our house was the third from the last on a dead-end street, everyone felt safe with me remaining on the front porch all morning.

Our neighbors sat on their porch all day too, I believe they looked over occasionally to see if I was alright. I found different ways to entertain myself throughout the day until lunch time. We did not have a key to our house so my brother would take me to the side of the house where I climbed inside through an open window to let them in the front door.

I remember so vividly the times when my oldest sister tried to make cornbread pancakes, but they never tasted like my mothers. We always had to pick corn weevils and mouse droppings from the cornmeal first before she fixed them.

After making our own syrup by heating sugar in a skillet and adding water we gobbled the cornbread pancakes down. My siblings then walked back to school again. And there I was, alone again left on the porch until their return after school.

By the time next semester came, I was old enough to start school, but I had already developed a bad stuttering problem; so, the teachers thought that I was mentally deficient.

The school decided to enroll me into slow learning classes where we colored and drew pictures all day, but I was thirsty for knowledge. Knowledge that I longed for but was not getting, and no one cared!

But being a little boy amongst adults, I didn't have a choice. Unfortunately, my mother was not strong enough to intervene on my behalf, but I know in my heart if she had known she would have.

I had a best friend that was the same age as me, named Paul. We shared the same interest in pets and games, but we also shared something else... allergic reactions!

"Hey Paul, here's a lot of blackberries for us to eat!"

"Oooo, thanks! I like blackberries."

No one told us that we had to wash the berries before we ate them, so we picked and ate them. Before long, our mouths started to itch. I ran into the house and told my mother what we ate, luckily, we didn't eat a lot of them. That was our first and last time eating those berries.

I remember having to go shopping with my father for the first time, the incident is still seared in my mind like a brand from a branding iron to this day. I can remember all the colors in the store and the many food items being so psychedelic.

As a young boy my mind could not digest what my eyes were asking it to do, the reds, the blues, the yellows, and the whites; my mind was numb from data overload. I always thought a grocery store was a drab place where you stood in a long line to order items like salt, flour, corn meal, sugar, and corn flakes.

Imagine my surprise when I saw all the different cereals on the shelves. This was too much visual data. I did not understand why there were so many different brands of cereal.

I wondered what they all tasted like because no name brand Corn Flakes was the only cereal I had ever tasted.

Hesitating from touching the boxes of cereal I did not know that I could. I ran from aisle to aisle looking for my father, then I spotted him eating shelled peanuts from a barrel.

My heart sank, I got so scared because I thought for sure we were going to jail. Instead, he offered me a peanut. I accepted the peanut as if it was a sacrifice, but I could not wait to get out of the store and back to the reality that I was familiar with.

Mom was very religious, she instilled in us to know the difference between right and wrong, and to go to heaven to treat people with respect, kindness, and goodness. If you did not follow those rules, surely you weren't going to heaven.

As a child I had a vivid imagination. I imagined in heaven everyone wore white because there was no dirt to get you dirty and you were always happy because you never went hungry. Life was always peaceful, and you never ran out of games to play with your friends.

I thought Hell was a sad place; this is where you went when you did not listen to your parents and did things, which you knew were wrong. You were thrown in scalding hot lava and the devil would stick you with his pitchfork as you cried out in pain for your mother.

When I witnessed two men die tragic deaths a few weeks apart, as a young child, that's when I realized there were other ways of dying other than old age. I originally thought everyone died peacefully in their sleep when they were 80 years old.

My aunt died from falling backwards through a window, she severed many arteries and bleed to death. From that day on, I promised my mother that I was going to be a doctor because I didn't want anyone else to die.

After returning from her burial, my family met over her house to eat a big meal, but I didn't understand why we had to do that.

"Mom why we eating a big dinner? It's not Sunday."
She looked at me and smiled, *"We eatin' away her sins."*

I looked around at all the people in the small house and was puzzled. I began thinking here I am trying to be good and keep my nose clean from going to hell and now I must eat her sins. That was the hardest food I remember having to swallow.

I was not afraid to die, just afraid of having to endure the excruciating heat and unrelenting pain and agony if I went to hell. When I prayed, I begged God not to let me die before I was able to explain what I knew about heaven and hell to him. I thought if I presented a good case, he would let me go to heaven.

As I grew older, I worried about going to hell less and less. Even though I worried less about it, there were things in the military I did that would justify me going.

I can't pick the specific time in my life, but I gradually assumed more and more of the provider role for my family, despite having an older brother and two older sisters at the time. Even though I assumed this role, I still felt that certain family members rejected me because of the color of my skin.

I was the darkest one out of my brothers and sister. They took on the trait of having a lighter skin complexion because my father's side of the family was Native American Indian.

I always felt that I had a special bond with my mother; I would look into her eyes when she talked to us kids and see how hard life was for her. When no other brothers and sisters were around, Mom and I would sit and have deep conversations about life and why things were the way they were.

Even to this day, none of my brothers and sisters are aware of some of the conversations we had. I played hard as a kid with my friends, but I also did everything within my childhood power to help mom raise the others. And even though we did not starve, there were many, many days that we went hungry.

I remember one day walking slowly from a house with a burlap bag draped over one shoulder as if I was being led to the gas chamber. I had taken vegetables from a garden, which was not ours because my brother and sisters did not have any food to eat. Even though I was only 9 or 10 years old, I struggled with the decision to take the vegetables.

That evening, I did not eat any of the vegetables because I knew what I did was wrong. I was so afraid of going to hell for what I did that I was willing to sacrifice myself.

I did not tell anyone where I was going because my parents would have stopped me. How could I? My mother taught us the difference between right and wrong and I knew what I was going to do was wrong. As I dragged the burlap sack down one row of vegetables and up the other, I tried to justify that what I was doing was the right thing to do. I only gathered enough vegetables for that night's evening meal.

It was difficult for me to pay attention in class when I was hungry. During recess, I would drink plenty of water to keep my stomach quiet in class. There were many times, I felt as if I would pass out from hunger, but I managed to survive this period in my life.

One of our classroom assignments was to write down what we ate for breakfast. I was too embarrassed to admit that I didn't eat anything, so I thought about food I had seen on a television show and wrote it down.

There was waffles, pancakes, eggs, milk, juice, toast, and sausage. The teacher began calling kids to stand in front of the class to read what we had written. After hearing those five kids had the same breakfast, she asked,

"Did anyone have anything other than the waffles, pancakes, eggs, milk, juice, toast and sausage?"

No one came forward or raised their hand. What did she expect? She should have known that we all were poor.

My clothes were Goodwill issued and my shoes were not the best. I was not into brand-named clothes, however in grade school I would have loved to have a pair of name brand jeans, because other kids had them. I knew we were poor, but it really hit home when the other kids in school pointed and laughed at the cowboy shirt I wore often.

"That's a pajama shirt you're wearing!" one kid pointed and laughed.

"Why would I wear a pretty shirt like this to bed? I picked this shirt out myself."

I then lightly touched my sleeve to show him.

After a few other kids asked me the same question throughout the day, I realized that it WAS a pajama shirt. I never wore that shirt back to school ever again, only around the house.

I must admit, of all the hardships I encountered in my life, the Christmas holidays affected me the most. It hit me hard in my heart from leading up to the showcase afterwards.

As an adult, I knew I was going overboard buying for my children. I knew deep down inside that the fire engine I bought my son was the one I always wanted as a child. Each item had to be wrapped in Christmas paper, no matter how small, mainly because my gift as a child was wrapped in newspaper.

Don't get me wrong, I was very grateful for what we received. Christmas day was the worst but also the best of times. One year, I walked out to the vacant field that was close to our shotgun house, laid down in the tall weeds, and asked God to take me.

Surely, I was a bad boy because Santa did not bring me anything for Christmas again. I do not know how long I laid on the ground, but after realizing that God was not going to take me, I walked back home.

Sometimes I stayed in the house all day because I did not want to see the gifts my friends received for Christmas and having to admit I did not get anything.

I can remember one year on Christmas Eve; Dad took us to the military armory to receive a present from a fake Santa. Once again, my pride got the best of me. I did not want to give the satisfaction of walking up to the fake Santa and giving him the pleasure of seeing a little boy begging for a toy at this poor kid's toy handout activity.

I knew I was poor, but I would rather not get a toy than beg for one. So, I to walk up and thank him, my father was so upset but I didn't get a whipping.

Most of the children in school were poor, but the teachers gave us an assignment of writing to Santa asking for gifts, which we knew he would not be bringing on Christmas day.

When you are poor, you learn early that Santa was mom and dad. We had the Christmas programs each year with teachers sending home a list of items and what clothes everyone should wear in the program. We were all poor! Didn't they realize that?

Ms. Williams, my fifth-grade teacher, had a dislike towards one girl named Jane, because Jane's mother was outspoken whenever Ms. Williams did something she did not like. One day in class, Ms. Williams asked each student to bring an item to make a cake.

"Do you think your mother can afford to send a pound of butter Jane?"

The next day, Ms. Williams asked each student what their parents had said about bringing in an item. Then she asked Jane what her mother said. With a gleam in her eyes and a smirk on her face, Jane responded,

"Ms. Williams, my mother said she not sending you a damn thing!"

Ms. Williams peered over her glasses with her mouth gapped open in shock. We all snickered because of the curse word Jane said. Ms. Williams then began shuffling her papers nervously as we all began laughing. From that day forward, Ms. Williams stopped picking on Jane.

I remember when my youngest brother, Jacob, had a part in his 1st grade Thanksgiving program. The night of the program a terrible snowstorm was starting. The snow was at least 2 to 3 feet deep and still falling.

"I have to be there, no one knows my part." Jacob said as if he was about to throw a tantrum.

He crossed his arms, one over the other and poked out his lip to pout. I didn't want to disappoint my brother so me and two of my older sisters agreed to get him to the school program that night even though we had to walk.

It was horrible! The snow froze our feet, the cold winds ripped right through the lining on our coats. We felt like icicles by the time we made it to the school, which was 4 miles away and we were chilled to the bone. We managed to get Jacob to his class just in time and we stood in the back of the cafeteria where the program was held.

We saw Jacob walking with his chest out, happy, and proud as can be. You would think he was going to win a big award for his performance.

Everyone in the cafeteria was quiet as each kid delivered their speech and now it was Jacob's turn. He beamed with excitement as he took one step forward and said,

"We are the turkeys!"

And then he took one step back.

"Wait what? That's it?" I asked as we looked at each other and couldn't do anything but start laughing. We walked four miles in the snow and near froze to death to hear him say four words. To this day, we still joke about this.

Neighbors

The first neighbor I will talk about is Reverend Williams, who was a preacher that grew the best watermelons in the neighborhood. Reverend Williams spent each day caring for and tending to his garden and he paid me a few pennies for pulling the weeds from his garden. I always admired the large watermelons he grew.

One evening when my friends and I were hanging out in the field, they noticed the big watermelons in Reverend William's Garden. Originally, I did not want to participate, but his watermelons were so tempting so we took a few to eat.

The next day as Reverend Williams worked in his garden, he noticed some watermelons were missing. As I continued to work on his garden, he was frustrated and said,

"Whoever is taking my watermelons better stop, if they don't, I'll have a surprise for them."

I could tell by the look on his face, he knew my friends and I took them, but we chose not to heed his warning. That evening we took more watermelons from his garden, only this time there was a difference after we finished eating them. Within an hour, our stomachs began to churn fiercely.

"*I got to go home!*" one of my friends said as he wiggled side to side. My other friend held his stomach as he doubled over and began sweating profusely,

"Joe Louis, we'll see ya' tomorrow!"

They began running home. Everyone was trying to make it home, turns out we all suffered from diarrhea so bad that we practically laid awake all night running back and forth to the bathroom.

The next day when I was working in the preacher's garden, as he slapped his knee and bent over with a loud hearty laugh he said,

"I wished I could have seen the thieves who stole my watermelons."
"Why you say that Reverend Williams?"
"I split the watermelon vines with a knife and added diarrhea medicine. I bet they had a awful time last night."

As he continued to laugh hysterically, I excused myself to run as fast as I could back to my house to use the outhouse. My friends and I never took any more watermelons from his garden again.

There was a witch that lived at the end of our street, well she reminded us of a witch because she looked just like a character we saw on television.

She lived alone in a huge one-story house. One day me and my cousin sat in the field in front of her house and wondered what kids in the neighborhood she was cooking. My cousin stood up as I tugged at the bottom fold of his blue jeans to make him sit back down.

"I'm going to go ask if she need any chores done."
"Don't go! She will put you in a cage for dinner!"

He left from the field and walked to her front door, once I saw him go inside her house, I debated should I rush inside the gate to look for my cousin or should I run home to tell mother?

After waiting for what seemed like an eternity, I built up enough courage to enter the witch's yard. Slowly pushing open the heavy metal gate, I stuck my head in first to look around in case I had to run.

Since everything looked okay, I entered her yard. Moving fearfully, I was determined to find my cousin. I walked to the house to knock. The witch opened the door, but I stood their speechless. I did not hear her speak but she knew why I was there.

"He's in the back of the house, you can go where he is."

I thought it was a trick so that she could put me in a cage too. I took one deep swallow and began walking to the rear of the house with her following me. To my relief, my cousin was picking up items off the floor and setting them on shelves for her.

"Oooo... can I help?" I asked as my eyes lit up.

"Sure, you can help him."

I no longer thought of the cage, which I perceived waiting for us, I was thinking about the money we would make from working.

After we finished, she paid us 25 cents each and sent us on our way. I later met up with my friends and told them what happened, but no one believed me.

I don't know why we never performed another job for her, she gradually over time became the witch again.

Directly across the street from the witch lived a rich lady, and her house was one of the prettiest on the street. It was surrounded by a white picket fence, and two smaller houses.

This lady was always so mean to us. Maybe it was because we always played in the ditch outside her fence or because we dug holes into the side of her elevated yard. We even use to sneak into her yard to look around at all the things she had.

Across from our house lived Mr. Evans who was an inventor. I called him an inventor because there was never a piece of junk he could not mold or retool into something else useful. I would watch in fascination as he mixed and made bricks to extend his house.

Mr. Evans lived alone but he never asked us to go to the store for him neither did we ever see anyone visit him. He rode a bicycle throughout the city, and he laid brick for rich people.

We were all afraid of him because he never smiled or allowed us to get close to his property. We always played baseball in the open field near his house but if a ball went into his yard, he would never give it back.

There was another inventor two houses down from Mr. Evans named Mr. Adams who also lived alone, but his house was the opposite of Mr. Evans. Mr. Adam's house and yard was filled with old washing machines; that was how he made his living; fixing washing machines.

His yard was like a washing machine cemetery. you would see machines be unloaded at his house, but rarely see any leave. His hands were as rough as leather, but his clothes always smelled of oil. Unlike Mr. Evans, I would occasionally sit with Mr. Adams and talk about life.

Everything I know about cars is because of one neighbor named Mr. Dooley who had two metal legs, but I don't know how he lost his real legs. He was able to stand but not walk.

Mr. Dooley could put his ear to a running engine and determine what was wrong with any car. When I saw his car pull in his dirt driveway, I always ran over to his fence so that I could watch how he got out of his car without walking.

When he opened the car door, he would push it all the way back, then he would take his left hand and grab his left leg as he lifted and swung it out onto the ground. He repeated the same steps with the right leg. Mr. Dooley grabbed the roof of the car next as he pulled himself up to lean on his car door. Navigating from the side of the car leaning on whatever was available, he eventually made it to his front door.

Family Pets

My family loved dogs more than any other animal; they were treated as if they were part of the family even though they ran free, and we did not tie or lock them up.

Running free meant our dogs had to find their own food. As a child I did not realize how much was involved with taking care of animals. Hardly anyone in the neighborhood except the hunting dog owners bought dog food for their dogs. We were barely able to buy food for ourselves.

There were abandoned pets running around the neighborhood whose owners could no longer care for them, those dogs formed packs for survival. It's a wonder no kids were hurt or killed by them.

During one of our treks around the farmer's wheat fields, we saw two dogs running wild, they were so glad to see so they played with us. The male was black and white, and the female was brown and white. But I do not know if they were, abandoned or if they walked away from their own home.

The two dogs followed us as we hunted rabbits in the fields. They followed me home, so I named them He-dog and She-dog. Even though He-dog and She-dog stayed with me, they were still loners, not getting too close to anyone. One morning, I went outside looking for them and just like that after one week I never saw them again.

Eventually I got my own dog that I named Bullet. He was my first true pet that I loved, and the feeling was mutual because we bonded immediately. Bullet needed me just as much as I needed him, because he filled a void in my life at the time.

Wherever I went Bullet went too. He knew when I was sad and lonely. He used to lay his head on me until the loneliness left my eyes. When he sensed that I was in danger he would nudge me to let me know to be careful. I showed him off to the other boys in the neighborhood all the time.

On rare occasions, you would see the city dog catchers trying to capture the abandoned dogs. These occasions were like a carnival, because the catchers chased the dogs as they tried to run away, we ran behind the dogcatchers. I remember the catchers caught one little, small dog which was too petrified to run from them.

One dog, which we named Sore Neck, terrorized the neighborhood. There was a wire slip noose around his neck, which over a period had cut deep into its neck.

Whenever Sore Neck came out of his hiding place, we all would run away as if he was monster from a horror movie. I knew he was hurting because of the huge gash around its neck, which is why I hoped he would stop running and let the dog catchers catch him. Bullet always made sure that Sore-Neck never came close to me or our house.

The local police were always patrolling the neighborhood and they watched Bullet as he grew. One day while I was playing outside, a police car stopped in front of our house. He got out of the car, walked up to my father, and began talking.

Bullet and I were keeping one eye on them as they talked. The policeman and my father started to walk toward us, and Bullet started growling. We both sensed something was not right.

"How you doing son? That sure is a fine dog you have there."

The police officer said as he tried to pet Bullet; but Bullet wouldn't let him and pulled away.

"He would make a fine police dog; would you want to sell him?"

Dad told him that Bullet belonged to me and that he would have to ask me. The policeman turned back to me and before he could repeat what he wanted,

> "NO! I will not sell him for a million dollars!"

I was serious and I believe the policeman could tell I was. He stopped smiling, turned, and walked towards his police car. But before driving away, he looked back at me and Bullet and had a smirk on his face.
    I kneeled in the dirt, hugged Bullet even tighter than I ever had before and said,

> "Don't worry Bullet, I won't let anything happen to you."

A few days later I got up early to play with Bullet. He was always there waiting for me to come outside, but this morning, he was not there.

> "Bullet...Bullet...Bullet!"

I called and called his name, but he never answered, and I was devastated. I cried until no more tears could fall from my eyes. I wondered how could I live without Bullet? Frantically, I searched everywhere for my dog, my best friend, but I never saw Bullet again.
    I did not want to believe that the Policeman took him, but I knew he did. Every time I saw a police car, I would walk up to it and hope in desperation that my dog would be inside.
    I was so lost, my dad even tried to offer other puppies, but no dogs could replace Bullet. People say you cannot die from a broken heart, but I believe this was the closest point in my life when I thought I would die from a broken heart. I have not called another dog my own since Bullet.
    One early Spring Day to our surprise, my mother brought home a cute baby duck. This duck gave us a reason to smile and get up each day because it needed us. Mom told us that we needed to raise the duck for Thanksgiving.

But at the time, I did not comprehend what that truly meant. We fed it scraps of food, corn, and any wheat we were able to salvage, that spilled from the trains passing by.

What a unique pet! All of us kids fed and played with the duck all the time.

"Do not name that duck!" Mom said.

We promised her we wouldn't, but as the duck grew, we eventually gave him the name, Wilbur. This was no ordinary duck, because it did not have other ducks to pattern itself after, it began running with our dogs. Wilbur chased other dogs and even tried to bark; he even became the protector of our yard.

As Thanksgiving grew closer, Mom warned us again that the duck, now known as Wilbur, would be the main course for the Thanksgiving dinner. We refused to even consider eating Wilbur. How could we? He had become a family member.

The day before Thanksgiving arrived, all us kids surrounded Mom begging and pleading with her not to kill Wilbur.

Mom did not want to admit it; but she had grown fond of Wilbur also. On Thanksgiving Day, all of us kids, He-dog, She-dog, and Wilbur ate roasted chicken instead. Wilbur lived a long life afterwards and died of old age.

My Street Family

Whenever a human body was discovered in my neighborhood, everyone would converge where the body lay as if they were coming out to see a circus. Death was one of the common elements which brought people together.

The first body I discovered was a man lying in the large vacant field at the end of our street. At first, I thought the man was asleep in the weeds, so I slowly tip-toed up to him and stood over him waiting for him to awake.

In the beginning I made a little sound but to no avail, so I made louder sound, and the result was the same.

I hesitantly approached the body even closer to look down at his face and he looked so peaceful. When I finally realized he was dead, I ran to my friend's house that had a telephone and told him what I found.

His mother called the police as we ran back to the dead man's body. We circled the body as we waited for the police and ambulance to confiscate the body.

The police arrived before the ambulance attendants and started to examine the bullet holes in the dead man's chest. They were cold, callous, and unemotional as they completed their examination.

By the time the ambulance arrived it looked as if everyone in the entire neighborhood was in the field watching how methodically the body was being prepared for transportation to the morgue.

After the body was loaded into the ambulance, the van slowly weaved through the mass of people who followed it like a New Orleans funeral procession. The ambulance slowly drove up the block turned left and disappeared.

"Let's go and sit on the corner to watch the drunks!" I said.

All of us walked up the block, turned the corner and to our surprise, the ambulance was parked in front of the neighborhood bar.

We made it just in time to see the attendants get out of the ambulance and go inside to drink a few beers before completing their trek to the morgue. This was the life I lived.

The surrounding neighborhoods were a melting pot of ethnicity. There were Germans, Italians, and a few Mexicans. Even though there were no fences among the neighborhoods, all of kids automatically knew to stay within our own neighborhood.

It was beyond our wildest dream to receive a brand-new bicycle, so we decided to build our own. Each one of my friends scavenged for items we could use as bicycle parts. I was one of the last to get my bicycle built.

Even though when I rode it, my bicycle went up and down like a see saw because the wheel rims were oval shaped, I still loved having my own transportation.

One morning we all met in my backyard. We were feeling adventurous, feeling like Christopher Columbus with having our own bicycles.

"Did y'all hear about the pigeons in an old warehouse?" one of my friends asked.

"Pigeons? What they look like?"

"I dunno...but since we have bikes, we can go look at them in the next neighborhood."

We decided to meet up the next morning to make the trek to the next neighborhood a few miles away. Our neighborhood was separated from this town by at least four sets of railroad tracks and an oil refinery.

My friends and I wanted to capture a baby pigeon so that we would be able to show it off on television one day. Also, we wanted to test our bikes to see if they could endure such a long trip like this.

The next morning, we met at our designated staging area and ten of us started our trek. Before we made it to the first set of railroad tracks, our bicycles broke down.

You must understand the quality and shape of our bikes. We were just kids using sticks to hold wheels together, a piece of wood held down by a rope as our seats and whatever else we found lying around. My two friends whose bikes fell apart waved for us to continue our journey like we were on a military mission. Once we crossed the four sets of railroad tracks the nervous chatter among us was becoming less and less.

Then one more bicycle broke down, now there were seven of us left. As we were passing the oil refinery, the only sound we heard was the hissing of steam from pipes. This neighborhood was quiet, and there were no drunks or hobos hanging outside.

We began thinking maybe this trek was not a good idea, but no one wanted to say, Let's turn back. I'm sure we all would have without hesitation, but none of us wanted to say it. It was now 9:00 in the morning, as we rode our bicycles down the middle of the streets the people who were outside on their porch looked at us as like we were aliens.

This was a different type of town than what we were accustomed to seeing, it was 100% German, clean with no trash laying around, quiet, and the grass was green.

We had never been exposed to racism, but we were today. I can still recall the look on some of the resident's faces as they saw seven little black boys riding old, dilapidated bicycles down the middle of their streets.

When we realized that black people were not allowed in this neighborhood is when we noticed a few of the residents run into their home as we rode down their street. But we continued our trek to the vacant warehouse we heard had the pigeons.

Reaching our destination, we parked our bicycles and walked slowly towards the big warehouse without saying a word to each other. As we walked up to the entrance all types of birds flew out of the broken windows.

There were rusted machine parts laying around the ground and overgrown grass in the open field beside the building. The warehouse had become a dumping ground since it was out of business. We walked one behind the other and went inside. We soon spotted the huge beam where the pigeons were nesting.

"How we going to get up there?" I asked as I looked upward.

"I dunno. Maybe if we stacked some items, we could climb up top." a friend said.

As we were trying to determine how we would navigate up to the beams, two police cars pulled up to the entrance of the warehouse and got out of their car.

We were frozen with fright when they came inside. The police began accusing us of riding our bicycles to their town to steal.

"We didn't come here to steal anything out of your town, we wanted to see some pigeons!"

Then we all began talking at once.

"SHUT UP, you little niggers!"

We were then searched like we were already criminals. Not knowing how to feel, so many thoughts began running in my mind. Something is going to happen to me, and my mom won't know where to start looking for me. She won't know what happened to her baby boy. They roughed us up and then pushed us towards our bikes.

"Get on your bikes and get the fuck out of our town!"

So, we got back on our bikes and started our trek back to our neighborhood. We noticed that one of the police cars was driving behind us with the lights on, as if making a statement to the townpeople saying, we caught them, and they won't be coming back to our town ever again.

After my initial fear wore off, I imagined we were returning adventurers and that we had a police escort showing us off. I even waved at some of the townspeople who came out to see what all the commotion was about.

When we saw the railroad tracks in sight, we all peddled as fast as we could to cross them. The police car did not cross the tracks, they sat there with the lights still flashing.

The policeman got out of his car and stood beside it. He put his hand on his hips and pointed at us. We were at a distance where it was obvious, he began shouting profanity at us, but we could not hear or understand any of the words he was yelling.

We stopped pedaling and turned our bikes around to look at him, we felt a little braver now because we knew he would not cross the train tracks. We began yelling back at the police.

"Yea, why don't you come across the tracks to our neighborhood?" one of my friends yelled.

We watched as the police turned their cars around and drove back to their neighborhood, as we continued to ours. We were now hungry and thirsty, so I went home.
"Where have you been?" my mother asked me.

"Nowhere, just riding with my friends having fun."

Surviving and learning street smarts occurs over time. One of the main rules of the street is to keep your mouth shut to never say a word about anything you may see.
My neighborhood consisted of a six-block radius and every aspect of my adolescence happened within these six blocks including the events from the local bar in our neighborhood called The Club.
Since we were not old enough to enter The Club, we spent hours sitting across the street from it at one of the vacant houses to observe the comings and goings.
We knew the names of all the regulars and what they were known for. There was Snake, Big Buddy, Buddy Shaw, and Match Thrower who was a little too friendly with the kids.
The Clubs patrons were mostly older adults, except on the occasional Friday or Saturday night when a DJ would spin records which brought in a hand full of younger patrons.
The neighborhood also had a store located in the same building as the club and owned by two sisters. The store could hold approximately seven people at a time, single file. It sold basic home items like staples, lunch meats, sodas, cookies, and candy. That was all that made up my six-block neighborhood.

Mom and Dad were World War II babies; they did not have much faith in the banking industry. My mother used an empty milk can that she sat on top of our wood-burning stove to dry out. The burnt milk left a foul smell in the can, which the money absorbed too.

"Joe Louis, I need you to go to the store and get me some eggs and milk."

My mother said as she handed me a list along with the foul-smelling money.

Off to the store I went, but before arriving at the store, I tried to fan the money in the wind, rub it in dirt, and even rubbed weeds on it just to get rid of the burnt milk smell. When I reached the counter and handed the dollar bills to the store owner and he asked,

"Where do you get this awful money from?"

I was so embarrassed when she asked because I was only a child, I didn't know any better. I tried my best to get the smell of it off, but it didn't work.

My street family consisted of primarily five boys my age. They were called my street family because even though we were not related, we were close as brothers and provided the emotional support and companionship that we did not get at home.

Hughie was an only child, and we were all a little jealous of what he had. His mother bought him the best shoes, the best clothes, and toys. We gathered at his house just to hang out.

Our fathers never sat down with us to talk about relationships, girls, or sex. Those were topics you never talked about or learned from your parents.

We learned our sex education like every other boy, we read the Playboy magazines that one of my friends stole from his father. We huddled around one magazine at Hughie's house one day to look at the all the pictures.

Hughie's was the house of choice when we talked about girls. I don't remember what kind of job his mother had but he was home alone 90% of the time. Of all my friends, he was the most obsessed with girls, he was always trying to look and smell good for them.

One morning we met up at Hughie's home. I walked on the porch and knocked on the door. Unexpectedly, is mother came to the door.

"Is Hughie home?"

"No, he's sick and in the hospital."

When we saw her wipe her eyes with the tissue she was holding after closing the door, we did not ask what was wrong with him, she believed that he would return home the following day.

Several weeks had passed before we ever saw Hughie again. His mother saw us walking past the house and called us over to the yard.

Hughie then walked outside holding one arm and dragging his foot. We did not know how to react when he first came out of the house.

He was paralyzed, had a hard time speaking, wore a large shoe and had a metal brace on his lower leg. Hughie suffered a severe stroke at a young age. Even though Hughie could no longer run and play with us, we still took him along with us.

Apple Jackby (pronounced Jack-bee) was another member of the street family, that chewed tobacco. He was considered our leader; he thought of things for us to do each day. Apple Jackby had more sisters than any of us.

"Hey Joe Louis, you want some soda?"

"Sure!"

He handed me the bottle; I was so thirsty. It was a treat to be drinking a soda. Suddenly Apple Jackby bellowed over with laughter once he saw one drop of the liquid slide into my mouth.

"I used that bottle to spit my tobacco in!"

My stomach churned as I threw the bottle on the ground.

Little John was the muscle of the street family and was as strong as an ox. Many times, we got out of fights just by having Little John with us.

I met Little John long before becoming part of my street family. He gave me my first knock down drag out fight. When Little John first moved into the neighborhood, he stayed a few houses down from mine.

I had built a wagon that my friends pushed me up and down the street. We all stopped when we saw Little John peddling his new fire truck down the street toward us. The closer he peddled his wagon towards us, the larger he became.

The other boys and girls were now standing behind me because Little John and I had locked eyes as he headed straight towards me until his engine bumped my wagon. Neither of us said a word as we sized each other up and down. He was bigger than me, weighed more than me, and even had muscles as a kid.

Without saying a word, Little John reached down, scooped a handful of rocks and dirt in his hand and threw it in my face. He then turned around, peddled his fire engine truck back up the street and disappeared in his yard. The kids brushed the dirt from my face as one of them said,

"Are you gonna get him?"

"Yeah, are you gonna go get him?" another sounded off saying.

All eyes were on me, everyone waited for me to respond.

"Ummm... yeah."

How could I not go to his yard? My honor and pride were at stake.

"We'll push you up to his house to get him."

They all began pushing the wagon as if we were on a death march. Then the wagon stopped in front of his house. There was an elderly man sitting on the porch.

Surely, he's not going to let us fight I thought. Slowly I got out of my wagon, opened the gate, and entered Little John's yard and yelled,

"I'm gonna get you!"

I held my fist up as I walked toward him, but instead of telling me to go home, the elderly man shouted,

"Go kick his ass Little John!"

I stood there frozen as Little John leaped off the porch and on me. Within seconds, he had me on my back and sat on top of me. He began hitting me on the forehead as he scooped dirt with his free hand and poured it on my face. It didn't hurt because John wasn't really trying to hurt me.

I turned my head towards the fence and noticed my friends who pushed me to Little John's house, were standing on the other side of the fence yelling for me to get up.

"I'm trying!" I said as I kept kicking and pushing him.

I did the one thing you shouldn't do in front of your friends, I started to cry from anger. This was a good thing because I got a rush of adrenalin and was able to flip Little John on his back. When his grandfather saw that I had his grandson on his back, he ran off the porch and as he began pull me off him, he said,

"Get out of my damn yard!"

His grandfather picked me up and tossed me to the side, then angrily yanked Little John up by the arm of the ground.

"Boy get yo ass in tha' house!" he said pushing him in the back.

As I walked out the yard, the kids brushed the dirt off me. I then got back into my wagon as they pushed me back down the street. I felt victorious afterwards. They didn't say anything about me crying.

"You were getn' ready to really get em' Joe Louis."

"Yeah, I was!" I said smiling.

After some time, me and Little John became good friends.
    Next was Snooky, who was Little John's little brother. He was the jester out the bunch. Anything that happened in our street family; Snooky always laughed hysterically. He had a high pitch laugh that was continuous.
    Finally, there was me and I was the voice of reason for the group. If at any time one of our treks seemed not to be a good idea, I always explained why we shouldn't do something. Most of the time everyone in the group agreed.
    Our neighborhood archenemy was a family by the last name of Howard. There were over fifteen children in this family, and every one of them was mean and nasty including the girls and parents.
    No one, in the neighborhood associated with the Howard's because they always intimidated everyone. The Howard's picked fights with everyone for the most insignificant reasons and the police were constantly at their house.
    My street family had to remain vigilant, so we never went anywhere alone.
    One day, my mother asked me to go to the store to get a bag of baking powder. This was one of those rare occasions when none of my street family members were around to walk with me, so I had to go alone.
    After making sure members of the Howard family were nowhere to be seen, I ran as fast as my legs would carry me. When I arrived at the store, I noticed all the children playing in front.

I looked around to make sure there were no Howard's among the children playing, with my eyes focused on the store door I darted from behind the bushes and ran as fast as I could navigating my way through the children.

Even though I was only in the store a few minutes, it seemed like hours. The whole time I was thinking I got to get out of here before the Howard's decided to come to the store.

After I got my baking powder but before I went outside, I put the bag in my pocket to make sure I did not lose it during my mad dash back home. I stood inside the door of the store and took a deep breath before I went outside. I opened the door, stepped outside, and notice nothing but silence.
Something was wrong! I thought.

The children were no longer playing or laughing, they were standing in a semi-circle in front of the store's door. I stood there a few seconds looking at each one of them when one of the Howard's stepped out from among the crowd.

His name was David; he was the most vocal of all the Howard's and the one who did not hesitate to start a fight but rarely ending one.

Before I could re-enter the store, some of the children blocked the door forming a fight ring around David and I. Fight or run? I had never run from a fight, and I was not going to start.

Normally when David starts his verbal tirade, another member of his family would intercede and that would be as far as David needed to go.

But this time, there were no other Howard's around, and David realized he was in a dilemma, but we were both committed to whatever transpired from this meetup. As he looked into my eyes, he knew I was not going to run and said,

"I'm gonna get you Joe Louis!"

As he got closer and closer, I made the tightest fist I could, as if my life depended on it. With no words spoken and with one punch I hit David on the nose with all the strength I could muster.

"Ahhh! You broke my nose!"

David stopped, stunned, and hurt. He grabbed his nose as bright red blood began to spurt everywhere. We were all shocked at the sight of so much blood pouring from his nose. He tried to stop the blood flow by holding his sleeve up to his nose, but it wouldn't stop, it kept flowing.

David started to hyperventilate and became delirious at the same time. He began to smear the pouring blood from his sleeve all over his face. He then picked up a piece of cardboard that was laying on the ground by his feet, raised it to his nose and wiped blood on it.

The sight of blood on the cardboard and all over David's face frightened the other children, they ran away. David looked at me turned and ran home. I was right behind him, I wasn't chasing him, I was running home that was in the same direction. After David ran past five houses he stopped, then turned and faced me.

"I'm gonna get you Joe Louis!"

That day never came, David never messed with me again.

Chapter Three

The Stories That Shaped Who I Am

There were many stories in my early life that affected the way I lived my life. Even to this day, I still say you can always learn from any situation both good and bad.

This saying is a direct result of my life's experiences. I chose the following stories to write about because these are the ones which had the most dramatic effect on me.

School Again

In the early 60's it was no guarantee that you started school at the age of six. Sometimes, children did not start school until they were seven years old. So, getting into school was difficult for me, because I was born at home, and either the midwife forgot, or deliberately did not record my birth at the courthouse so I had no official birth certificate.

During the beginning of each school year, my brother and I got two pairs of jeans, two shirts, a package of socks and a package of underwear. Based on how big the holes were in our tennis shoes determined if we would get a new pair.

I do not know what would have happened to me if it was not for my new first grade teacher. I was nine years old sitting in the first grade with seven-year-old classmates. She took me around and introduced me to the other teachers.

There was an audiologist and a speech teacher the school sent to my house. Eventually, I was diagnosed with having a severe stuttering problem. The school also sent a nurse out to my house occasionally to see how we were being raised. I never forgave my previous first grade teacher for making me spend two years of my life in special education classes when the only thing wrong with me was stuttering.

In my new school, we had a catered lunch in the classroom.

"Always leave a little food on your plate… it is proper etiquette."

"But what if I'm still hungry?"

She gave me a polite answer and I understood what she was trying to say, but I was still hungry every time we ate lunch, so I did not leave any food on my plate.

In school I did everything possible to excel academically. I always tried to score higher than most of my classmates on tests which made me feel good. Now I had something that no one could ever take from me even if I was poor; it was my knowledge.

I was not the best dressed or the best fed, but I was one of the smartest kids in the class. Taking tests and scoring 100% was the norm for me. I noticed when the teacher walked up and down the aisle passing out the graded tests, she would give me mine with a 100% written in the right corner and not say a word to me.

But when the other students who received less than a 100%, the teacher would smother them with attention. So, I thought if I missed one or two problems, the teacher would give me some attention too.

The big day approached. As the teacher handed out the math quiz, my mind went into overdrive. What type of problem was I going to miss? I struggled trying to find a wrong answer, it was new territory for me. I never struggled with trying to find a wrong answer, which the teacher would believe.

The next day, she placed each student's test on their desk, and leaned over to show what was wrong. I waited impatiently for her to pass my test back to me. My heart pounded as she kneeled to put my test on my desk.

"You know how to add better than that! You got lazy and did not pay attention what you were doing!"

Wait, what happened to the smothering words? I wondered. The motherly attention? The pep talk I know you can do better speech. I received nothing, and I never purposely missed a test question ever again.

"I know you can do better than this Joe Louis, you know how to add!"

The Spelling Bee

I excelled at spelling because it came natural to me. One day, I asked my mother and father for a Webster's dictionary for Christmas when other little boys asked for guns and toys.

I begged and pleaded all year long. When Christmas arrived, my mother handed me a big, brown, paper bag... I quickly went to my special corner, ripped open the bag and there inside was my Webster's dictionary.

I was so happy and excited that I immediately laid on the floor and started to consume the contents. I loved everything about my new book, even the pictures that were in black and white.

At school, I enjoyed going to the black board to take spelling quizzes. I always raised my hand because I was starving to show that I was smart as or smarter than the other kids in the classroom.

Theotis, one of my classmates, was always reluctant to go to the board because he had a difficult time spelling. He struggled with spelling his name even though it only contained seven letters. When the teacher looked away, I wrote his name in small letters for him to see and copy. He and I became good friends after that. From that day forward, whenever we had spelling test, Theotis always stood next to me.

When the yearly spelling bee championship rolled around, I was always one of the participants with my entire class cheering me on. The spell off was now down to me and two other students and it was my turn to spell.

"Spell the word modernization."

In my head I knew how to spell it, but I wanted to show off in front of my class. I began smirking as I spelled the word, but I was spelling too fast.

"Modernization, M-O-D-E-R-N-Z-A-T-I-O-N."

I then looked at the judge.

"I'm sorry, that's incorrect."

I was stunned, my heart sank. I then realized that I left the letter I out of the word. As I walked back to my classroom with my head down, I felt as if I let the whole world down. How could I face my classmates after this? I thought. To my surprise, no one gave me a hard time. The spelling bee was not talked about.

Hidden Symphony

I always marched to my own drum while in grade school. Unlike other little boys I loved symphony music. Once a year, my grade school was given the opportunity to attend the symphonic orchestra that costed 50 cents to attend. I would save all year so that I could attend. However, in my neighborhood, there was a code; the symphony was something only girls attended not boys.

I had to do strategic planning with how I would get to the bus that would take us to the symphony. The first detail was to determine the clothes I would wear.

Even though the teacher told us to wear our Sunday best on that day, I knew that would be a red flag if the other boys saw me in those clothes. Instead, I wore my clothes that were a little better than my day-to-day school clothes but not as good as my Sunday clothes.

The second detail were the shoes. So, I put my good shoes in a paper bag and wore my tennis shoes to school. Then I changed into them before loading the bus. I was able to sneak outside without any of my friends seeing me getting onto the bus. I leaned low in the seat so that no one could see me, I was relieved when the bus pulled away from the school.

It took us an hour to get to the orchestra. The show wasn't in East St. Louis, but was in the neighboring city St. Louis, Mo. When we reached the entrance there were so many white people standing out front. I had never seen that many white people before and they all were nicely dressed.

"Okay, kids we're here!"

We were so excited that we started bouncing up and down on the school bus seats.

"Listen kids, I need everyone to get off the bus and line up by the front door and remember to be on your best behavior."

As we got off the bus, I would wonder why everyone was looking at us. The people pointed, whispered, and looked at us as if we were from a different planet. It reminded me of when and my friends took that bike ride to see the pigeons and how everyone came on their porch to look at us.

Once inside, we had two chauffeurs that showed us our designated place to sit. I sat in awe the entire time I was there. Each year after, I did the same routine all over and none of my friends ever found out.

The Principal from Hell

In grade school, the one figure that struck fear in all the kids was Mr. Johnson, our principal. He was a large, intimidating man that towered over all of us, and he had a deep, booming voice to match.

He had a strict rule that restricted us boys from goofing off on the girl's side of the playground during recess. And as usual, my boys and I had to play on the girl's side of the playground just because.

One recess out of nowhere, Mr. Johnson was supervising the girls' playground when he saw us.

"Hey, you nappy headed boys...you shouldn't be on this side of the playground, come here!"

Quick as a flash, we all ran to the boy's playground and tried to blend in.

"I know who you are!"

"Joe Louis, do you think he know us?".

"I don't know."

We got in line trying to blend in with all the other little boys. But to our surprise, Mr. Johnson was standing at the door staring and scanning each boy as they passed by him.

Mr. Johnson was so tall every child had to look up to see him. He had dark circles under his eyes, short grey hair, and he always looked as mean as possible.

My friend was ahead of me in line, and I watched as he passed Mr. Johnson staring. As Mr. Johnson reached down and pulled Charlie from the line my heart skipped a beat because I knew the rest of us were dog meat.

James was next, but as he passed Mr. Johnson, he did not get jerked from line. Now it was my turn. As I took tiny steps forward, I felt his eyes glaring and burning through me, but I did not look at him. I felt my heart pounding through my chest as I stood a few steps in front of him. I could not stand it, I wanted to jump out of line and throw myself at his mercy, but I didn't.

As I passed in front of him, I paused ever so slightly waiting for him to jerk me from the line. I got pass Mr. Johnson without him jerking me from the line. Twenty minutes had passed before Charlie returned to class crying from the whipping Mr. Johnson gave him.

Snitching was something me and my friends never did on each other. Charlie told the principal that he did not know who the other boys were. That day we escaped Mr. Johnson's wrath.

I was always testing Mr. Johnson and his rules.

For example, he had a rule of no one being in the school building during the lunch recess. But I forgot something in my homeroom that could not wait until after lunch.

I made stealth moves through the empty building, making sure no teachers saw and especially not Mr. Johnson. I navigated the first floor without being seen; I managed to pass the second floor but on the verge of walking up to the third floor I heard a booming voice from behind, it made my blood turn to ice water.

"Hey boy come here!"

I froze, hoping that Mr. Johnson was calling someone else,

"You...I said come here!"

I didn't turn around, I saw him out the corner of my eye so that he wouldn't see my face, but I wondered about what to do.

Without further analyzing the situation I took off running down the other set of stairs and out the door to the playground. After the lunch bell rang, and we all were marched back into class, my friends told me that they heard Mr. Johnson was visiting each classroom looking for the boy who ran from him during lunch. It had become the buzz of the school that afternoon.

"Oh Lord, take me now."

I stared at the clock as it slowly ticked away each second which seemed like hours. The only thing I thought about was having the home time bell ringing and me running home hoping Mr. Johnson wouldn't catch me.

"Mr. Johnson is on the third floor. I wonder who he lookin' for?"

Charlie did not know I was the boy he was looking for. The home school bell rang before Mr. Johnson made it to my classroom. I felt a sigh of relief as I rushed out of school towards home.

My neighborhood was five miles from the school but when I got closer to my block, to my surprise and horror, Mr. Johnson was walking towards me with his wooden paddle. I stood there waiting for my punishment. Mr. Johnson walked right up to me, pointed his paddle in my face and asked,

"Have you seen a boy named Fred?"

An answer to my prayer, Fred did something in the school, that made Mr. Johnson forget about what I did. I was smiling ear to ear.

"No sir, I have not seen him."

I responded and finished walking home.
When I became an adult, I learned that Mr. Johnson had two children that could not wait until they were old enough to leave his house because he treated them just like he treated his students. I drove past his house one day, I saw him sitting in his wheelchair as he stared out the picture window, watching the world pass him alone.

Meat Cleaver Chop

My neighborhood required certain survival skills, which carried over into school. I had entered Junior High School, but I still felt that I needed a weapon for protection. My weapon of choice was a meat cleaver, which I carried in the waistband of my pants and a set of brass knuckles. To maintain the element of surprise, we did not share with each other the type of weapon we carried.

One morning Johnny and I were walking to our Junior High School, when we passed by our old Elementary school. We knew there was morning roller skating in the gym, so we decided to peek inside and watch the kids skate just for a few seconds before we continued to our school. Johnny slowly pulled open the outside door to the gym, not noticing the male teacher standing on the other side of the door.

As soon as the door was wide enough to exit, the male teacher hit Johnny in his chest with enough force to make him double over and go down on both knees. The teacher then started walking towards me, I thought to do the same thing.

But I startled the teacher and myself with the amount of speed I used to pull the meat cleaver from my pants. I grabbed the teacher's arm and held it to show him I would use it if I was forced to. The teacher snatched his hand back and held both arms in the air surrendering.

Still holding my cleaver, I reached down with my other hand and helped Johnny up but never taking my eyes off the teacher. We continued walking to our school, never telling anyone what had happened.

The Hole

Every day in grade school was a constant struggle trying not to let the other kids know how poor we really were even though most of the children were.

During the school year, we only got one pair of shoes and it was up to us to make them last the entire year. That was one of the reasons I pulled my shoes off after school and was barefoot during the evenings and weekends.

I tried to take care of my shoes as if they were alive. Using only water, I cleaned the dirt off to the best of my ability, and I would walk lightly when I had them on.

But one day while examining my shoes, I had to utter the five words every kid hated to say, "a hole in the shoe." Finding a hole in your shoe required entirely different dynamics to fix it.

The kind of material you put in your shoe was based on the size of the hole. If it were two holes then you used torn pieces of newspaper, but if it was more than two you had to be creative.

The next day when I arrived at school, I waited in front of the building for my friend Charlie.

"Hey Charlie."

"Hey Joe Louis, what's up?"

"I have a hole in my shoe, and you gotta help me get through school today."

"No problem, you did the same for me before."

The first obstacle were the stairs. As a mass of kids were going up the stairs, Charlie made sure that he walked behind me at the right distance to keep anyone below him to see the bottom of my shoes. Even walking down the stairs required a different stride. There was a technique to walking with holes in your shoes, and we mastered it.

Each time the hole increased, I learned how to determine what piece of material to use for the holes by calculating its life span. If a piece of cardboard was used then it would last through six classes, a lunch period, and six flights of stairs. But by the end of the day, your ankles will throb from having to continually pick your foot up.

After a couple of days, my mother was able to buy me another pair of shoes from the local dry goods store which was rare during the middle of the school year.

Wearing the new pair of tennis shoes to school made me feel invincible, so I wanted to race against all the other boys who had old shoes on, and I won every race.

Even though they looked like everyone else was wearing, there's no telling how old they had been sitting in the hardware store.

I couldn't wait to play basketball during our gym period. I was the first one on the gym floor with my brand-new red tennis shoes on. I started to play as if my life depended on it. I was running up and down the court, stealing, passing, and rebounding, like a kid possessed. But all good things eventually come to an end. As kids started to focus on and watch me play, I decided to go up for a rebound.

As I was going up, someone accidentally stepped on the back of my shoe.

The higher I got into the air for the ball, I noticed that the top of my tennis shoes went with me while the sole remained on the floor. As I came down with the ball, the top of my KEDS was spinning around my ankle.

I picked up the sole of my tennis shoe and ran off the floor. Surprisingly, no one made fun of me afterwards. They were more amused at my ball handling performance.

The teacher allowed me to go home after gym class. As I walked in the house, Mom looked at my shoes and did not ask me how it happened.

I could see in her eyes thinking how she was going to get another pair of the tennis shoes from the hardware store for me. That embarrassment turned into something positive later.

Each year students were allowed to replace teachers for a day. The teacher would pick a student to teach or function in their capacity. To my surprise, I was chosen to be the principle. My family was so proud of me. Dad let me wear his dress coat and tie, even though the coat was too big.

I sat in the principal's office doled out punishments and accolades. I was in pure heaven. That was until we had to come back to reality. It was Square Dance time in gym class. Up to this point, girls were considered to have cooties and us boys did not want anything to do with them.

How could the teachers think overnight we go from cooties to being able to hold their hand, smile, and swing them around? Some of the boys took a whipping instead of dancing with the girls. The girls were crazy! Before gym class, they would put on perfume. Why? For what? We still didn't like them.

On one week the girls were on the floor first and the boys had to go out on the floor and pick a girl. The following week, it was reversed. I always tried to pick a girl who was not the prettiest. That way, no one could say that I liked the girl I picked.

A Bucket

In my neighborhood you were either a bully or the person bullies picked on. Don't fight; always walk away from it. It takes a better person to do that.

Those were the words mom would always say to my brother and me. Primarily the words were for me because I was smaller than the other boys.

Since we did not have, what we call, city water we had to ask a neighbor who lived on the next block to get water from the water faucet which was located on the side of their house.

My brother and I took turns carrying the pails of water from the neighbor's house to ours. It seemed I was always the one who had to carry the water. Mom always said to my brother and me to turn the other cheek when the neighborhood bullies would taunt us. I promised I would always turn the other cheek when the neighborhood bullies would taunt us.

Whenever it was my turn to carry pails of water from our neighbor's house, which was over a block away, the weight of the pales would cut into my fingers, and I would cry to myself in pain.

When the bullies would see me walking with the pails of water, they would make fun of me and pick up hands of dirt and throw in the pails, which I carried.

The bullies thought I was afraid of them because I never said a word or fought back. They did not realize I didn't fight back because I promised my mom I wouldn't.

On one occasion when I was returning home with the pails of water, the bullies pushed me, which caused most of the waters in the pales to waste.

When I did get home, mom noticed there was only a small amount of water in the pails and dried tear streaks running down both of my cheeks. I never cried; the tears were from frustration.

As my eyes began to fill with water again, without saying a word, I turned and ran back to where the bullies were as fast as my little legs could carry me. The boys were surprised that I was back so soon.

"Hey you! Repeat what you said to me a few minutes earlier!"

And just like that I fought and whipped each one of them, afterwards I slowly walked home.

"Do you feel better after fighting?"

"No, I just wanted the boys to leave me alone."

Those boys nor any other boys ever bothered me again.

The Whack for the Outhouse Cat

Mr. John's mother lived in a small house on his property next door to us and her name was Ms. Cole. I would wait in our backyard for her to come outside, hoping she would ask me to do some minor chores for a few pennies as payment.

Those occasions that she did ask, I eagerly agreed and sprinted into her two-room house. Ms. Cole's only companion was a large alley cat, which hated me, and I hated it.

I swear whenever the cat was alone with me, it tried to scratch me, which it did on a few occasions. I did not know if the cat did this to me only or to anyone who entered Ms. Cole's house. I put up with the cat because I needed the choirs to make a few pennies. When Ms. Cole returned to the room, the cat would sit next to her with an angelic look on its face as it looked at me.

If I ever met you outside, you are mine! My eyes said to the cat. A week later, I got my wish. The cat escaped from the house. Ms. Cole was hysterical; she asked all the neighborhood kids to help find her cat.

Lucky for me and unlucky for the cat, I found it. As I held the cat, I thought about the few times it scratched me. I thought what I could do to get even with it. I did not want to hurt it, just pay it back for the scratches.

We had an outdoor toilet, and it was one of the hottest days of the summer, so I had a brilliant idea. Put the cat in the smelly toilet! I did not think beyond the act, I did not think about how to get the cat out. I just wanted to pay the cat back.

I took the cat into the outhouse and held it over the hole. It started to meow loudly as if saying I am in here! Come and save me from this horrid little boy! I did not realize how agile the cat was. As I tried to push it into the toilet hole, its legs spread across the hole and held fast. As I pushed on the cat's back, it meowed louder and louder.

I hesitated a minute because I was beginning to change my mind. Suddenly the cat let go and started to fall.

I immediately felt remorse for what I had done. As I peered down the hole, I felt a slap on the back of my head.

"What you dun' boy?"

My dad was furious! When he saw what I was doing to the cat but could not get to me fast enough to stop me. I turned to face him.

"Nothing,"

As dad peered down the toilet hole to see the cat meowing, he barked again.

"You put cat down there, you git 'em out!"

"You want me to climb down in the toilet?"

I truly thought dad was going to say yes. The smell was horrible. I wanted to throw up but was too afraid to.

"The cat will die if you can't get 'em out."

Now I truly was sad and remorseful for what I had done. What I did, to the cat spread like wildfire through the neighborhood. All the neighborhood kids and a few adults gathered along our fence to watch the show.

As I tried different options to get the cat out, none of them worked. I did not know why the cat would not grab the rope I lowered to it.

As I left the outhouse to get other objects to get the cat out, the neighborhood kids laughed and made fun of me. Finally, dad rigged a clothes hanger contraption told me to stand aside while he fished and finally hooked the cat.

Before he pulled it out, he asked me to go into the house and get rags to cover and clean the cat. I ran into the house, grabbed a sheet, ran back into the outhouse, and passed the sheet to dad to cover the cat.

Afterwards, he gave me the wrapped cat. As I left the outhouse everyone started to cheer when they saw the cat. Ms. Cole was frantically pacing as I handed the cat to her.

Before I could get away from the laughing kids, dad caught and whipped me with a switch in front of all the kids. I did not cry but I hid my face on the ground and did not get up until all the kids had left.

I do not remember if it took them 2 minutes or 2 hours to go away. Ms. Cole never asked me to do chores for her again.

Sweet Berries

An elevated train trestle was on the other side of the road by our house. The trestle was made of concrete and fifteen feet high but looked 200 feet. On the other side of the trestle was a train switching yard that had continuous activity 24 hours a day, seven days a week.

It reminded me of an ant farm; trains coming and going in every direction constantly. A concrete tower majestically watched over the train yard; turning night into day with its strobe lights, the tower orchestrated the arrivals and departures of the trains.

What an impressive sight this was.

"You wanna go across the tracks and eat berries before dad get home?"

"Yeah! Let's go!"

We crossed the train tracks and stayed alert for anything coming our way, but we were so determined to taste the berries that grew wild on the concrete trestle.

Our father warned us about crossing the tracks alone, he said it was too dangerous, but we thought we could do it without him ever finding out.

We had a few close calls when Dad almost caught us; however, the sweet taste of the grapes was too great for us to stop. One day, our luck ran out. We stood close to the tracks and were too busy arguing about who would watch for Dad, that we didn't see him coming.

"Hey, what y'all doin ovr there?"

Too petrified to run, we stood there waiting to feel his wrath. Dad walked over to where we were standing, I was sure we would get a whipping, but we didn't. Instead, he reached in his pocket and pulled out a penny.

"This gonna happen if y'all keep playin on these tracks."

He laid the penny on the tracks, and we waited in our yard while the next train passed by us. He then took us back to the tracks to where he laid the penny.

"This how flat the train will make you."

"But if we are flattened, how will you tell us apart?"

Dad however did not see the humor in my question.

Hog Greed

Mr. John, our next-door neighbor, did not raise children, chickens, or a garden; he raised hogs and pigs instead. Hogs always intrigued me. They were big and sloppy. One day while sitting outside watching the hogs with Mr. John, I asked,

"Mr. John, why do they smell so bad?"

"Because Louis, they are not able to sweat and they wallow in the mud which has table scraps, hog crap, and stagnant water."

Mr. John then threw another bucket of slop on the ground. As I balanced myself on the wooden and wire fence Mr. John built, I watched the hogs and pigs for hours.

"If you fall into the pigpen, the hogs will suck the meat from your bones."

I believed him because I watched the way the hogs sucked down their food.

"Mr. John why is that hog so big? He can't walk."

"The bigger it is, the more money I get for it."

As I continued to watch the hog each day, all it did was lay around and wait for its next feeding.

"Mr. John, you better sell that hog or butcher it 'cause it's getting too big!"

Mr. John didn't say anything, he kept on working in the yard. Each week Mr. John gave the surrounding neighbors a pail to collect their table scraps. It was so nauseating watching Mr. John taking each pail of scraps and hastily pouring the contents into the pigpen.

This hog was so disgusting because it ate all its meals laying on one side and siphoning garbage into the side of is mouth, all while wheezing for air and grunting because it did not want to share the garbage with its pen mates and smacking due to a lack of teeth.

Sitting on the fence as I watched the hog one morning, I noticed the hog did not look right. So, I jumped the fence and began running toward Mr. John's front door yelling,

"Mr. John, Mr. John, your hog looks funny!"

The door flew open as Mr. John sprinted out towards the hog pen, still pulling up his overalls and I was right behind him.

"What's wrong with the hog? Will it be okay?"

Word traveled fast in the neighborhood about the hog that everyone came to see it. Mr. John was rushing to slaughter his hog before it died. He was losing the opportunity to either sell it or lose the meat.

Mr. John, and a few neighborhood men had to hurry to get the hog to the neighborhood slaughterhouse as fast as possible. They tied the hog, which was laying on a wooden door to his truck bumper and dragged it to the slaughtering area.

The slaughterhouse was not too far from Mr. John's house, so I ran there as they were loading the hog, because I wanted to be there for when they arrived. I watched the men initiate and complete the slaughtering of the hog.

Once or twice, I had nightmares about the hog driving the train and blowing its whistle as it ate garbage and chased me around our yard.

Sunday Chicken Dinner

If we had to raise hogs, it would have been okay since I was accustomed to the smell of Mr. John's hogs, but we didn't, we raised chickens like our neighbors.

Excluding the smell, chickens were more aggressive than the hogs. They fought constantly for food, water, shelter and sometimes for no apparent reason.

We had baby chicks and hens. The baby chicks were so cute when dad first brought them home in a box, little did the chickens know we were raising them for food.

Me and my brother helped dad construct a securely covered hen house that was easy to enter, easy to exit for food and water, and provided easy accessibility to their nest.

I felt so bad chasing the hens off their nest to take their eggs, apologizing for taking their babies for us to eat. The chicken coop roof was built with wood planks we found in the junkyard and the frame was surrounded with chicken wire.

We had the meanest rooster I had ever seen, and it was the boss of our backyard. Even though the rooster intimidated the hens, chickens, and even us kids; he did an outstanding job keeping peace in the backyard.

Whenever the chickens fought, the rooster intervened, but when we played in the backyard, it always chased after us. My mother told us it was because we were playing in his territory. She always had to rescue us when the rooster blocked our path to the house.

I hated the rooster because it was mean and was always chasing us. I believed he deserved the same fate as the chickens did when one of them was chosen for Sunday's dinner.

One Sunday, after we returned from church, my sister was in the backyard by herself playing. Without being provoked, the rooster jumped on her head and cut it open with its spurs.

"Momma!"

When we heard my sister scream, we all ran out the house to see blood running down the side of her head. My mother grabbed my sister in her arms and took her in the house. She cleaned the wound, put gauze and bandage on her. My mother patched her up the best way that she could.

Afterwards, my wish finally came true. The rooster was about to receive the same fate as previous chickens did on Sunday. Unfortunately, it was time for me and my brother to complete the fate of the rooster.

"I hate this!" I feel sorry for the chickens 'cause they leave their babies."

When I had to behead a chicken, I always tied a blindfold around its head and tied its legs together.

But on one particular Sunday, I was lazy; I did not feel like taking the time to blindfold the Sunday dinner chicken. I went outside chased and caught one of the chickens. I then took it over to the chopping block where my brother was standing. He held the chicken down on the chopping block for me. The chicken began frantically waving its wings around and squirming around to get away.

"Hurry up!"

"Okay...okay..."

The force of the axe chopped the head off and immediately the head went one direction and the body the other direction. A steady stream of blood began squirting from the chicken's headless neck. I panicked and dropped the axe on the ground.

The headless chicken jumped, and its body ran around with blood still squirting from its headless neck. As I ran, I thought the headless chicken was chasing me for revenge because of what I had done, but eventually it finally fell to the ground. I didn't feel like eating chicken that day.

The Bee Catchers

Since I no longer did chores for Ms. Cole, I was free to assist Dad. My father never said no to anybody even if it was something that he did not know how to do.

I remember when honeybees built a nest in the loft of our neighborhood church; the deacon asked Dad to extract them. Dad agreed, which the Deacon knew he would. This is how my dad became known as the neighborhood bee catcher, and my brother and I became his helpers.

The three of us walked to the church with me pulling a little red wagon. The people in the neighborhood wondered what we were about to do.

But all we truly knew about bees were that they made honey and did not like smoke. The deacon waited for us, when we arrived, he let us in and immediately left.

"Dad what should we do?"

"Hold the stick…let me light it and give it to your brother."

Dad started to prepare the can, once he began sticking cotton onto the stick I was holding, he then lit the cotton.

"Ughhhh this stinks!"

"Give it to your brother."

After I gave my brother the stick he climbed up to the nest of bees, he waved the stick back and forth in front of the hive. My dad then climbed up the ladder after my brother finished and attempted to cut the hive down.

"Joe Louis, move the wagon close to the church wall."

Once I put the wagon in position, Dad threw the hive down. There were some bees still swarming around the hive but not as many. We then walked back to our house.

It must have been a spectacle for everyone watching us walk down the street pulling a little red wagon covered with bees and still fanning other flying bees with the smoking cotton stick. We were stung several times until we became numb to the stings.

Dad was always creating something, so he built small boxes to put the bees in hoping they would stay. Most of the bees stayed and settled in on their new location.

Whenever we wanted honey, we would walk outside to the backyard, light a cotton stick and smoke the bees until we grabbed the portion of honey we wanted. Well worth all the stings we endured to have fresh honey.

Chapter Four

Getting Ready

Western Union

During my first year of high school, I worked evenings at my cousin's Western Union business on a teletype machine, that spewed messages from a gummed strip of paper.

After sticking them on a blank Western Union form, I then logged in the message for delivery. I was completely oblivious to the Vietnam War at that time because it only affected me when someone from the neighborhood never came back.

Each day the driver grabbed a handful of letters and out the door he went for delivery. One day I decided to read one of the messages, but they were all the same except for the soldier's name, address, and when they were killed in battle. This had such a profound effect on me that I can still remember the first few words, 'We regret to inform you that your son was killed or wounded in the Republic of Vietnam.'

I felt this was a cold and insensitive way to notify a family about the passing of their loved one. At first, I thought getting the letters ready was the worst part of the job until I had to deliver them.

On my first day of training, we pulled up to a house in the evening time. The driver slowly walked up each step and proceeded to knock on the wooden door.

"Who is it?"

I heard an inquisitive woman ask from behind the door.

"Western Union..."

Pause... then there was silence.

My trainer told me to prepare myself because when the words Western Union are spoken, more times than not, all you will hear next is crying and yelling through the door before anyone opens it. Families automatically knew that a Western Union was delivering a death letter from the government.

A loud no from the core of the woman was heard several doors down. Next thing I saw was all the women from the neighborhood shuffling down the dirt road to the house. The lady never opened the door, so the driver left the letter in a crack. I did not have the stomach to continue delivering messages to these families, so I quit.

In April 1969, I received my draft notice. I believe America was galvanized against the war because of the protest at the Democratic National Convention. Many people felt the same way about our involvement with the war, which led me to write "The Radical Anthem" as my way of a silent protest.

Even though it was my silent protest, I was left with no choice but to go.

The Radical Anthem

My eyes have seen the coming,
Of these wars that's taking place.
Losing honor for my country,
Better yet the human race.
Inflicting pain upon my brothern'
Taking that what is rightfully theirs
These wars shall continue on
Glory, Glory hallelujah

Poked and Prodded

I was nineteen years old and had never been anywhere further than 50 miles from where I was born. I did not know what was about to happen, or what I was getting myself in to. On the day it was time for me to leave, I got up extra early because I had to catch a bus to the Induction Center, in St. Louis, Missouri.

I was surprised to see my mother also got up and stood outside as I began walking to the bus stop. I kept turning around to see whether she was still watching me or did she go back in the house. She didn't leave that spot, she watched and waved until I turned the corner and was out of her sight. I was truly alone now.

When the bus pulled up and stopped, I readjusted my suitcase in my hand and climbed up to have a seat. I began thinking this may be the last time I will see my neighborhood or my family.

"Good morning, Sir, could you tell me if I'm on the right bus? I need to go to the Induction Center."

"This bus will take you across the river... sit in the front so I can tell you where to get off."

As the bus rode over the bridge, I stared at the total darkness of the Mississippi River and began feeling fearful. Fearful of the unknown, fearful that I wouldn't see my family again, fearful of what was in store for me.

As the bus driver pulled up to the bus stop, he motioned for all the other passengers to get off and then he turned to face me.

"Son, you must walk five blocks West and then three blocks South to get to the Induction Center."

"Thank you so much Sir."

"Good luck Son! "

We shook hands but he held it a little longer as he looked me directly in my eyes. I got off the bus, it was still dark outside as I walked West. I tried to remember everything and everyone that I passed to formulate a mental picture of what I was leaving behind, every man and woman etched in my mind as if I would never see them again. Block after block I continued my journey.

"Hey Mister, you have a quarter?"

I reached in my pocket without saying a word, I gave the homeless man a quarter as he sat on a bench surrounded by his entire life in a shopping cart.

"Thank you and God bless you Mister," he excitedly said as he put the quarter in his torn shirt pocket.

I walked the five blocks west and as I turned the corner to walk the remaining three blocks South, I saw that I was not alone. Young men, such as I, were on both sides of the street walking.

We were like homing pigeons being navigated to a destination by the forces of our papers to the Induction Center. Some of us exchanged nervous greetings, a few paired up, and others gave a head nod acknowledgement as we continued to our destination.

At first, we were lulled into thinking it would not be bad, as we were provided a hot, fresh, breakfast and then a lot of instructions about what would happen over the course of the next few days. Some of the soldiers flew in from different states, so the instructors were easy on us the first day.

The second day is when everything changed, and reality hit us hard in the face. Early in the morning, the instructors barked commands at a mind-boggling pace. Our bodies were moving, but our minds were trying to wake to begin functioning after a deep sleep the night before. Half of us stood in lines with our clothes on while the other half stood in lines with their clothes off.

We were probed, thumped, twisted, told to squat, walk on our tip toes, to turn our head and cough, and to breath in and out. At our expense, some of the instructors thought of different ways to torture us mentally just to have their fun. I stood at attention to the clinic room entrance anxiously waiting for the next set of instructions.

"Get in here and sit in the chair Private Loveless! "

A tall and muscular man stood in the doorway yelling at everyone. His muscles were bulging out of his shirt as he seemingly peered into your soul.

As I hesitantly sat down in the chair, the medic walked over with a grin on his face and holding the long needle up in the air,

"I have to give all of your shots in your neck."

I began hyperventilating, but I had no choice. I couldn't run and I wouldn't cry, so I sat there trying to prepare myself mentally and physically for the pain I was about to receive. The medic then wrapped a large rubber tourniquet around my neck and began snickering with the muscular drill sergeant.

They thought it was amusing watching me panic as my butt rose from the seat and my body tensed up. After a few minutes he took the tourniquet off my neck then proceeded to give me the shots in my arm.

I had never seen other people naked except my brother and cousins, so it was awkward. The gruff drill sergeant made us stand so close that our bodies touched. I could feel the hot breath on the back of my ear lobe, and the chest hairs on my back from the person standing behind me.

The smell of unwashed human flesh, the image of naked out of shape men, and their closeness was more than I could bare; I wanted to vomit.

Any soldiers that became sexually aroused because of close contact were immediately pulled from the line and led away, never to be seen again. After all tests were completed, we all stood in the day room waiting for the drill instructor.

"Get in line according to your height!"

The muscular drill sergeant once again was yelling at us, but we all scrambled to get in formation according to our height and then we popped to attention. As drill sergeants began running in the room yelling at each person. This was the day we dreaded because it was the day that determined our fate.

Into the room walked representatives from the Marines, Army, Air Force, and Navy.

The Marine Sergeant went first glancing right over me because I only weighed 112 lbs. he had no use for me. He wanted the biggest and meanest men, so he began calling names to step forward.

Next, the Army Sergeant called his set of names, and I was one of them. I was told that if I went Army, by signing to do an extra year I would significantly reduce my chances of going to Vietnam. Boy was I naïve!

We had to wait until the following day to find out where we were going for advanced training. We stood nervously at attention in line as our name and destination for basic and advanced training was announced.

The beat of everyone's heart throbbed so hard you could see their chest going up and down. The sergeant called the code for Vietnam aloud and started to name each person chosen.

"Code 72B, Louis!"

I ran between a sea of soldiers to retrieve my paperwork. When I arrived in front of the Army Sergeant, I snapped back to attention and asked,

"Sir, what field is this?"

"Computers...now get back in line!"

I was ecstatic! I would not go to Vietnam instead I would be working on computers. We were then bussed to the airport together.

I had never flown on an airplane before; I was so nervous, but I didn't want to have a meltdown because there was a child sitting in the same row. It would be embarrassing having a grown man panic.

Fort Ord, California, here I come. After landing, drill sergeants were waiting for us inside the terminal, and they ran from every direction yelling.

"Get in line! Get in line! Get in line at parade rest and stay there until we tell you to move!"

There we were, at parade rest in an airport terminal until everyone was off the plane. Then we proceeded in a straight line to where the parked buses were located.

"Get on the damn bus, face the floor and don't say a muthafuckin' word!"

He was yelling at the top of his lungs because the veins popped out from his neck. The bus ride was excruciating long because we couldn't look or talk to each other. Pure silence!
Eventually the bus came to a stop and the sergeants got off the bus. You could hear them whispering as we remained sitting on the bus with our heads down.
Suddenly, we heard the thunder and vibration of boots rushing onto the bus. The sergeants went row by row yelling incoherently at everyone.

"Get off the bus, line up and look straight ahead! For the next eight weeks, I will be your worst nightmare, from this point forward you are MINE!"

In my head I thought I will not let them get the best of me; I'll show them. I knew the main goal of the sergeants was to tear us down both physically and mentally and then turn us into soldiers that obeyed orders without the slightest hesitation.
 It seemed as if they kept focusing on me but I didn't know why. I was far from being the biggest or the meanest soldier in the camp.
Eventually I discovered the reason, it was because I was the toughest mentally. We weren't civilians anymore; we were becoming SOLDIERS! The other soldiers looked up to me because I never begged the drill instructors to stop whatever they were doing to me.
As a matter of fact, I asked for more.

One day as we were instructed to lay in a bed of thorns wearing nothing but our shorts I yelled,

"WETSUP!"

WETSUP stood for We Eat This Shit Up! Whenever we needed to cry out in pain, instead of begging for mercy, we all yelled WETSUP!

After eight weeks of trying to tear me down physically and mentally, the sergeants could no longer stand it. They promoted me and told everyone that I was the type of soldier they needed to strive to become.

Drugs

The Army was my first real exposure to soldiers abuse of alcohol in basic training. Because we were restricted to the base, I was surprised at the lengths some soldiers went through to get high. They would take white bread and pour shaving lotion through it then drink what was strained through the bread. On one occasion a soldier used melted shoe polish paste filtered through the bread as well. I did not want to partake in such activities.

One evening as we were sitting in the television room watching the latest movie, a fellow soldier walked behind where I was sitting. He slowly pulled a Bowie knife from his waistband and with one jolt forward he held it to my throat. With his left arm wrapped tightly against my forehead, he pressed the knife firmly against my beating and protruded carotid artery with his right hand. I was now a prisoner in his world.

"Bugs are crawling in my veins!"

His body started to shake, and his eyes began to bulge. The other soldiers stopped watching television and turned to watch what was happening.

"He put the bugs in me!"

We tousled to the right then to the left. I knew the soldier had a greater chance of slitting my throat before anyone could approach him, so they chose not to intervene. I began talking to the soldier about everything I could imagine to take his mind off the knife and me.

"So watcha' think about this food they serve us? I miss my momma's home cooking...what about you?"

"Wh-what?"

Confusion started to settle in, and I could feel his grip loosening. After an intense fifteen minutes of talking, he began to cry; I did not know if this was good or bad so I continued to talk about things that weren't emotionally triggering.

Someone called the military police, but when they arrived, they realized they too were powerless. The soldier had the upper hand in the situation, he could not be rushed because the knife was on my throat, and we were too far from the door.

I knew it was up to me to save myself. I continued to talk to the soldier as he went through different emotional stages over and over.

This ordeal continued for over an hour until he grew tired and succumbed to giving up. After throwing the knife to the door, the military police rushed in, tackled him to the floor and took him away. I grabbed my throat checking for any injuries as my adrenaline rush subsided.

The other soldiers went back to watch television, but I went to my bunk to lay down. This is the reason why to this day, I will never have my back turned to an opening; my back will always be against a wall so that I can observe everything and everyone entering.

Advanced Training

During advanced training, I became even tougher mentally and physically.

The sergeants treated us like humans, but we had structured routines each day; calisthenics, breakfast, class, lunch, class, and our evenings, though rare, were free so I began taking night classes. One evening my classmate leaned over on the desk and asked,

Are you okay?

He pointed to my arm as if he was looking at something in a horror movie. I looked down and began seeing bright red, raised patches developing. I became lightheaded and passed out. When I woke up a few hours later I was confined to an isolated portion of the hospital. I was housed in a small building separate from the main hospital in the center of the complex.

I began taking account of my surroundings, confined in a secure building with at least twenty other soldiers. The doors were always locked as occupants were escorted to other departments in the hospital by military police whenever tests were required.

I was lying next to a soldier who was always handcuffed to his bed on one side, and one that was lying in a bed filled with ice on the other side. I could not comprehend what was happening and why I was being isolated.

I asked the attendants what was wrong with me but was never given an explanation. In the early morning hours medics always quietly rolled a gurney in as they stopped at each bed to read the name on the chart looking for a specific person. When they found that person he was always taken away. A few minutes later I could hear the soldier scream a few times and then there would be silence.

Every morning, I thought they were coming to get me next. I even tried to calculate the day based on the pattern of soldiers that were previously taken.

No one would answer my questions, so one morning I decided to move to another bed, because I was sure they were coming for me. And what I predicted to happen, did.

The attendants entered the ward pushing the gurney and went directly to the bed I was supposed to be in, but I was now laying in the bed across from it pretending to be sleep.

When they noticed the bed was empty, they looked at their list, shrugged their shoulders and took someone else. I never found out what they were doing to the soldiers.

The Loan Shark

Back then, the military frowned upon soldiers launching entrepreneurial endeavors while they were in uniform, especially when it dealt with money.

After I was released from the hospital, my life went back to normal as I returned to my training classes. I tried to think of things that I could fill my evenings with since I did not frequent the bars like the other soldiers because I was not a drinker.

We were paid very little so by the end of each month, many soldiers were broke. On one occasion I went to one of the bars off base with a fellow soldier named Chester.

I really did not want to go, but he begged me to come because he did not want to go alone. I watched the bar girls key in on which soldier they knew was weak and an easy target.

To my knowledge, Chester never had a girlfriend, so he was easy prey. As the waitress escorted us to a table, I could see her sizing each of us up and down to determine who would be an easier financial prey.

The waitress knew which soldiers to shower their attention on with offering an occasional free beer, an extra smile and a pat on the hand.

Chester fell in love with the barmaid fast and hard and began spending all his free time at the bar freely giving all his hard-earned money.

Many late evenings, Chester would stagger back to the barracks waking everyone up professing his love. Since I was not into bars or nightlife, I always had plenty of money.

Chester was disliked by the soldiers too because he hated to take baths.

One night the other soldiers decided to give Chester a blanket party, so they waited until he was asleep in his bunk, and then rushed over to his bunk and wrapped him in a blanket.

"Get off of me...let me go!"

Chester was tossing and turning trying to fight them off, but they were not letting him go. They struggled to get him to the shower, but once they arrived, they took turns scrubbing him harshly with soap. I felt sorry for him during formation the next morning, because his skin looked like a boiled lobster and was extremely red. He never spoke of that night, but he began taking showers after it.

The soldiers that drank and gambled their money away started to ask me for short-term loans. Even though I was growing tired of being treated like a lending institution, I decided to begin acting like one. I thought if I started to charge interest then that would deter the soldiers from asking for loans, but it didn't.

"Hey Louis, loan me twenty dollars again until payday. "

I was growing tired of Chester always asking me to loan him money, so I thought of something that I thought would deter him.

"I charge interest now Chester. I will loan you twenty, but you must give me thirty back... take it or leave it!"

To my surprise, he accepted the terms and conditions. I did not think what I was doing was illegal, so I bought a little black book to keep track of who owed me money and how much. My money loaning business was quite lucrative. I did not think my superiors would object if they found my little book.

By the end of the month, I was making more money than what I was being paid by the Army because I was loaning to soldiers outside my barracks. I kept my little black book inside my locker to help me keep track of everyone's payment.

During one of our random inspections, we were told to open our lockers and stand at attention next to them while the officer inspected it. The Lieutenant who was inspecting my locker grabbed the little book and thumbed through it.

He paused a few times as he read the names, seemingly to take a mental note of them. My book was confiscated, and I was ordered to not loan any more money.

"Hey Louis, you got twenty dollars to float me until payday?"

"I am out of the loaning business Chester; you need to make that barmaid fall in love with you instead of your money!"

From that point forward, he lived paycheck to paycheck.

The Voice

In 1970, I succumbed to peer pressure. My friends and I had a weekend pass, so we all decided to walk the strip. I've never been a drinker; so, I was always the voice of reason whenever we went out. But on this night, I decided to drink two beers while the other soldiers drank six each.

After leaving the bar, we walked along Chesapeake beach, watching the surfers being bashed into the beach sand by the ocean waves.

"Hey two beers, can you surf?"

Even though I was stumbling, the soldiers laid the surfboard that we found in the water for me as I laid on top of it. I dog peddled my 112lb body out into the ocean to meet the incoming water, but it wasn't long before the board was captured into the jaws of a massive wave. I nervously and timidly attempted to stand on the surfboard, but the beer in my system was preventing me from doing so. I wobbled on the board side to side as the force of the wave took me further away from the beach instead of remaining close to it.

I panicked because I could no longer see land only the water that surrounded me on all sides was my view.

I fell and as I hit the swirling water, the surfboard hit me on my head. Dazed and disorientated, the current pulled me farther and farther from the beach. Spinning like a load of laundry and tossed like a rag doll, I could no longer tell up from down.

I thought I was going to die because I was in a battle for my life.

"God help me!"

I cried out as my body submerged up from the water. My brain still had enough oxygen to control my body not to inhale, but it was a struggle because my lungs demanded air, as I was under water. This battle raged on for what seemed like hours, even though it was only for seconds.

As my lungs were about to take a victory breath, knowing it would put an end to my internal struggle, I fell into a trance. I inhaled but realized it wasn't forced, I felt total peace.

I was no longer struggling to survive, no longer struggling to breathe, no longer in any fear or pain. I looked down at my body as it gently swayed left to right under the water currents.

I was amazed because the peace that overcame me, made me realize that I no longer wanted to be a part of the body I was looking down at.

My body continued to float upward to a light that shined through a tunnel. Like a moth drawn to a flame, the light drew me in. I did not grieve for the family I left behind because I felt that I was on a journey.

Even though I did not have a physical form, I was made whole as I kept heading toward the soothing light. There are no words in the English language that could explain how comforting the light felt. I wanted to continue my journey and pass through the tunnel, but I was soon stopped by a still voice.

"It's not time for you to come yet."

"But I don't want to go back."

"You must...you must write."

"Write what? I'm confused."

"You will know what to write when it comes to you, and you will name it The Letter."

Before I could respond again, just like a flash I was back in my physical body. It seemed like an eternity before I finally broke the surface of the water. My head completely emerged from the ocean's depth, as a female swimmer grabbed me around my neck and swam towards the beach with me in tow.

After she guided me to the beach I crawled on my knees and hands from the shoreline then laid on my back. Within a few seconds, my fellow soldiers who talked me into surfing ran up to me with terror on their faces and sheer panic in their voice.

"You alright two beers?"

"Wh-Where is the woman who saved me? I want to thank her."

I gasped for air and coughed up the remaining water in my body, as they stood over me looking down.

"You must be delirious! There was no woman with you! The waves washed you up on the beach.."

I was puzzled and dismayed. As my fellow soldiers helped me up, we began walking back to the barracks; and we were all silent. No one ever spoke of that incident ever again. I know what I felt, I know what I heard, I know what I saw, and no one could make me see things any different.

Weeks passed and things went back to normal. I was now stationed at Ft. Huachuca, Arizona. Upon arrival, I was given a tour of the military base.

I was awed at the security measures taken to get in and out of the computer area where I would be working.

When I went through my computer operations training class, we were told that during our first assignment, we would be assigned an experienced technician who would be our mentor.

This did not happen. I was a member of a team who was responsible for bringing a new computer system online in 120 days. To make matters worse, we were going to demonstrate this new system to a group of high-ranking military officers.

Once we introduced ourselves, we began working on the daunting task set before us. I was responsible for developing the operational procedures, as well as demonstrating how the system works. The technicians and I worked feverishly to put the system together and to make it operational.

The day before the demonstration, the system still was not working properly, so we agreed to work all night to ensure the demonstration was a success. The next morning, we got dressed in our starched fatigues, ready for the demonstration. The system had been running for a few hours without failure and we were feeling confident it would not fail.

The system looked impressive with its blinking lights of many colors, shapes, and intensity. As we waited for the VIPs to arrive, I was joking and said if the system breaks down during the test, I will flash the lamp test a few times. We all chuckled.

The moment of the demonstration arrived, and a row of chairs were placed less than 10 feet in front of the system. We were all standing at attention and then it happened; the computer stopped working.

Fortunately, the only people who were aware of the system failure were myself and my team members. Sheer panic spread across their face as they looked at each other. At the same time, in walked the entourage with the General in tow. As they were being seated, my operations officer said a few comments and looked at me as if to say it's in your hands.

I stood in front of the General and gave my prepared speech professing the benefits of this system. But now the moment of truth had arrived about what I was going to do to demonstrate the system when it wasn't working,

I had to think fast. I had an idea to put the system in test mode capabilities and simulate how it should work; they would never know.

So, I walked over to the master console and took the system offline. I repeatedly pressed the lamp test button which made the pretty lights flash on and off. I then walked over to the tape reader and fed a 20 ft tape through it. As the reader read the tape, I again pressed the button to flash the lamp tests.

Whenever I did this, I had my back turned to the officers so they could not see me pressing the button. I repeated this act at several stations on the operating system and it was a success.

I then turned and gave the entourage my closing speech, as we waited for the General to speak. My fellow soldiers and I held our breath. He commenced to praise us for bringing the system online in a short period of time and showered us with kudos. That evening, the technicians and I celebrated. It still took us a few additional weeks to finally make the system operational, but the hard part was done.

All the soldiers were assigned to live in an old two-story World War II barrack. One weekend, we decided to buy cheese to eat and wine to drink. I do not remember all the details, but I was told after drinking an excessive amount of wine, I walked over to the barrack windows and started to break them out with my fist to see if I could break the glass without cutting my fist.

After I broke ten windows, the noise attracted the military police to the area for investigation. But before they arrived, my friends hid me and pretended that that they did not know who broke the windows. It was becoming known that me and any amount of alcohol did not mesh well.

When we worked the day shift, we had the weekend off, allowing us to go off base to explore what the town had to offer. One weekend, we all decided to go to Nogales, a neighboring city close to the Mexican border. I instantly fell in love with the language, the culture, and primarily the food.

As we boarded the military bus, the driver reminded us of when the last bus would be returning to the base. Throughout the night my friends and I were having too much fun to keep track of the time.

We had no thoughts about our 8am formation early Monday morning. After we realized that the last bus came and left, reality hit us as we wondered how we would get back to the base. We began walking back to the military installation with dress shoes on and our bodies full of alcohol.

As we walked along the lightless highway, every bush became a wolf, every mound of dirt became a robber, and every sound was a wild animal hunting us. We walked so many miles that we started to walk on the side of our shoes and our feet developed blisters.

Three hours later, a soldier heading towards the base graciously picked us up and let us off near our barracks. We were now sober, so we ran inside to get into our uniforms.

"Do you think we're gonna make it Joe Louis?"

"We will if you guys hurry up and change, don't waste no time talking!"

We had just enough time to put on our uniform and rush to get in formation. We stood at attention, seemingly for hours even though it was only 10 minutes. As we stood there, out of the corner of my eye I saw my friend beginning to sway.

The alcohol and no sleep were beginning to get the best of him. Suddenly, a loud thud was heard by everyone in formation. My friend had fainted and hit the ground hard.

Our superior officer let him remain on the ground until the formation was over. We all had our butts chewed that day for not abiding to curfew, rushing into formation, and the alcohol consumption. The officer handed our punishment to us, and we were assigned to mess hall duties.

We cleaned pots and pans on our feet continuously for the entire month as our punishment. I thought I was safe, the recruiter assured me that I would be. He had assigned me the computer career field. But it happened… what every soldier dreaded…I received draft orders to **VIETNAM!**

Chapter Five

VIETNAM

The next chapter is the most depressing time during my entire life. There isn't much dialog in this chapter because I leave some situations for your own interpretation.

This was a very difficult chapter to write and talk about. A lot of circumstances were left out in this section because of the detrimental effect it has had on my mental psyche.

I cannot bear the pain of re-living and telling some of the horrible acts we were forced to do during our time in Vietnam.

Some events I will NEVER speak of again; I choose to take them to my grave. I want your perception of me being a good, kind-hearted man to remain, not the killer I was trained and forced to be when I was young soldier.

Vietnam Hell

The military provided us the opportunity to go home and say goodbye to our family, but I did not want my mother to know I was on my way to Vietnam so I made my brothers and sisters promise they would not tell her where I as being deployed to. As the day of my departure arrived, my family waited outside for the taxi to arrive to take me to the airport.

Mom and I made nervous small talk as we waited for the taxi. I felt she had a feeling of where I was going but neither of us said anything about it. How could we?

America knew that Vietnam was the country where a good majority of mothers knew they were sending their son there to die. The taxi turned the corner and drove slowly down the street towards our house as if it was in a funeral procession.

The driver pulled close to the curb at our gate, got out, and opened his trunk for my duffel bag.

As he opened the rear door of his taxi for me, I felt as if a hearse was there to pick me up for my final earthly journey. Before I entered the taxi, I hugged my mother tight as I fought back my tears. Me crying is not the last image I wanted my mother to have or remember me.

I bolted into the back of the taxi so that she could not see the swell of tears forming in my eyes. I truly felt I would never see my family again. As the taxi pulled away from the only safety net I had known, I watched my family until we turned the corner.

After my leave ended, I was physically and mentally prepared to go to Vietnam, I had no clue what was truly in store for me. I had no clue that once I stepped foot on Vietnam soil that it would impact my life and those around me forever. I had no clue about the turmoil, pain, and nightmares that would plague me until my dying days.

The driver knew I was headed to Vietnam even before I said a word, because he had repeated the scene many times with transporting mother's sons to the airport. He looked in his rear-view mirror and said there was another passenger he had to pick up enroute to the airport.

He pulled in front of a white house that had dangling broken shutters and overgrown brush. A scantily clad female barely dressed walked out of the house and slid into the back of the taxi.

This was the furthest thing from my mind, I demanded to head straight to the airport and nowhere else. I knew many soldiers fell for their scheme and lost their money in the process. The barely dressed woman got out of the taxi and walked back in the house as the taxi driver pulled away and drove to the airport.

After sitting at the airport for about an hour, I was soon able to board my plane enroute to the jungle training site in California. Once I reached the top of the stairs, I looked back on American soil for one last time.

I believed this was my last moment of capturing a glimpse of freedom and of life. Tears welled in my eyes as I peered through the airplane window. To relieve the hurt in my heart, I wrote Sun Rise.

Sun Rise

A new day awakened by the morning sun
Rises from the mist
Engulf us with your presence!
Burn away the hatred from our hearts.
Restore our souls.
Nourish those who wait for you
As the evening mist is replenished by the tears
Of all the cries of sorrow felt for one another
We beg for another day as we prepare for today's end

Burning Feces

After landing in California, I flagged for a taxi and gave him the destination, Fort Ord. Once I arrived, I grabbed my duffel bag out of the trunk, swung it over my shoulder and began walking. I began observing the myriad of different soldiers there for training. Some were training with M-14's and others M-16's.

Those that marched in formation with the M16 were looked at with a tremendous amount of respect because we knew a large portion of us them will not return from Vietnam.

As we trained in mock Vietnamese villages every day, I was always petrified. The real-life simulations were confirmation that if you did not get it right here, you knew you would be dead in the real jungle.

I learned that the most important member of the platoon was the point man that led the patrol. Even though their life expectancy was short in the jungle, I felt an overwhelming urge to be that person.

There I was, a momma's boy, a computer operator heading to Vietnam to fight. I was so naïve believing the recruiter, he led me to think that I would do my entire enlistment in a clean, air-conditioned, computer room, that would shield me from having any parts of the war.

Hell, I enlisted in the Army an extra year to keep from GOING to Vietnam! I only weighed 112 pounds, but none of that mattered.

There we were trained in mock Vietnamese villages, now we're flying to real life. After several hours of flying, we finally landed in Vietnam.

We worked ourselves into a nervous frenzy because we were expecting to begin fighting immediately once the plane touched down on the runway. but that wasn't the case. Once we landed and began departing off of the plane, the smell of burning human feces and the humid heat was overwhelming and nauseating. My stomach churned as my gag reflex became more prominent with every inhalation of breath. I had never smelled burning feces before.

How can I survive here? Burning feces, the humidity, killing, always being paranoid, the fear ran rampant in my young mind. After getting off the plane, we were rushed into a military bus to be taken to the processing center.

"Listen up! As a precaution, all the windows on this bus are covered with wire mesh to keep anyone from throwing a hand grenade in. DO NOT mess with the damn wire mesh!" the bus driver yelled.

I had never been so nervous in my entire life. The thought of being killed riding on a bus played over and over in my mind. When the bus doors closed; the driver drove as fast as he could through the small villages. He honked his horn as he continued speeding and swerving past anyone stepping in the path of the bus along the dirt road. I held on to my seat for dear life until we made it to the base unscathed.

During the Indoctrination process, we were drilled about the difficulty of distinguishing between the friendly South Vietnamese who worked for us and the Vietcong who tried to kill us, but on some occasions, they were the same person.

As I walked around the compound, I stared in the eyes of each Vietnamese trying to distinguish whether he was a friend or foe. I was always on high alert and jittery 24/7. So much was ingrained into my head that I did not trust anyone.

Getting a haircut was the first requirement we had to do after arriving on post. As I stood in the makeshift barbershop, I quickly scanned the area and saw only Vietnamese working.

"Have a seat private!" drill sergeant yelled.

The barber and I made eye contact as I was trying to determine friend or foe. I cautiously sat in his chair, held my breath, and waited for a hand grenade to go off.

Without expending too much body movement, the barber positioned himself behind the chair and me without saying a word. Before being draped, the barber started to move my head side to side, but in my mind, I believed he was looking around to see if anyone was watching.

As he continued, he suddenly snapped my head to one side, and I heard my neck crack. I immediately thought he was a Vietcong trying to break my neck but had failed. I leaped from his chair like a bungee cord yelling at the top of my lungs,

"DIEEEEEE!!!"

I continued yelling as I turned to lunge forward, grabbing his collar with one hand, and punching his face repeatedly with the other. I didn't see the puddle of blood expanding on the floor from the blows to his head. I only saw red because I believed he was trying to kill me.

Several soldiers ran over to pull me off him, but I was determined to kill him for attempting to snap my neck. His arms flailed around wildly like a rag doll trying to break free, but I had a grip that could not be broken.

"Louis..Louis! Calm down man...calm the fuck down!"

Other soldiers were yelling as they grabbed me trying to pull me off him. It took several seconds to snap back into reality of where I was located.

I was hurriedly rushed out of the barbershop and back to my hooch as the medics came and tended to the barber. I did not get a haircut for many months following that incident. Whenever the sergeant told me that my hair was protruding under my hat, I bought a bigger hat.

As I walked around the camp, I took note of the type of boots being worn. The seasoned soldiers walked with a confident swagger, and their boots had splotches of white matter; they had been through many hell battles. I wanted my boots to look like theirs…that's if I lived long enough. Their boots were considered a badge of honor.

After living at the camp for a week, I was surprised how much the Vietnamese people did for the base camps. They washed our clothes, cleaned, burned feces, and did any other odd jobs. This is why I wrote Disillusioned after a week in this country.

Disillusioned

My eyes have seen the coming
Of wars that's taking place
Losing honor for my country
Even more for the human race
Inflicting pain upon my brethren
Taking what's rightfully theirs
But these wars shall continue on

Assignment

My first assignment was to work in the telecommunications van out in North Vietnam, close to the DMZ. The cardinal rule of Vietnam for all soldiers is to not get close to people. Because if a friend dies, you will lose your focus out in the field.

The next morning, I had my duffle bag ready to leave at sunrise. As I sat in the back of the truck, once again the driver high balled the wired bus through the villages. After a few hours the truck came to a screeching halt at a small village compound.

I stood up, pushed my duffle bag off the back of the truck then jumped down into a pile of clay dirt. I was overwhelmed by the desolation of this compound; I saw other soldiers scurrying around from hooch to hooch like rats scavenging for food.

Since no one came to greet me, I picked my duffle bag up and started walking around the compound. After determining where the makeshift welcome center was located, I was given my work assignment and the location of my hooch.

There were a few soldiers already in the hooch, but I was able to find a vacant cot. I fought back tears as I plopped down to de-stress after the long ride. I was now truly alone, scared, and in a foreign country. I always thought in my head, Lord, if it is your will that I die in this country, then let it be.

The next morning was a little better than my first. I walked around the small compound to acclimate myself. Clay dirt was everywhere…and in everything. As I trudged through it, I eventually found the communications van where I would be working twelve hours on and twelve hours off. I decided to walk inside to introduce myself. Afterwards, I walked back to my hooch and started to unpack. There was a soldier on the opposite bunk watching as I unpacked.

"Where you from?"

"A small place called East Saint Louis."

I didn't want to hold a conversation because I remember the cardinal rule of not to develop friendships, but I asked,

"How long you been in country?"

He looked down as he continued to flip through the magazine,

"A couple of months."

And just like that the conversation was over. He continued flipping through the magazine and I continued unpacking.

Death was closer to me than any of the other soldiers because I did not go through the typical Army training for a Vietnam soldier. Because of my small stature, I was forced to also train as a Tunnel Rat.

Tunnel rats were the soldiers that performed underground search, destroy, and kill missions. The tunnels contained supplies that we could use; however, they were also launched with surprise attacks, and some were even booby trapped, but it was my responsibility to crawl through them.

I settled into a routine of working twelve hours on and twelve hours trying to become invisible and mindless in a country where we did not belong. I always carried a throwing knife strapped behind my neck because when I was not working, I practiced for hours learning how to throw it.

I eventually became so good that I could reach behind my neck and throw it with deadly force and accuracy fifteen to twenty feet in seconds. I also carried a small hatchet strapped to my right side, and a machete, on my left. Soldiers were so afraid to pass by my hooch because they were petrified of getting hit by one of the weapons.

One day we underwent a surprise visit by a Senior Officer that flew in to see how things were going in Vietnam. As the entourage entered our communication center, the senior officer asked me how messages were logged on the routing slip.

I had been awake for almost thirty hours, so my brain did not process the question asked of me. I responded with you start at the top of the form and end up at the bottom. I was not trying to be funny I was mentally drained. Some of the lower grade officers snickered but this made the Senior Officer angry.

Two days later before sunrise, I was awakened to be told that I was now a machine gunner and tunnel rat and that I had less than one hour to pack my duffle bag. I was now being shipped closer to the Demilitarized Zone.

I was issued an M-60 machine gun and was not able to say goodbye to the soldiers I worked with. I jumped on the back of the transportation truck and headed further into North Vietnam.

Once I got to the area, I could tell that this was not going to be good being stationed here, it was less than 50 soldiers, and many of them were on a hard drug called scag.

I reflected to when I signed up with the recruiter to do an extra year to keep from going to Vietnam, now here I am in Vietnam…at one of the worse duty assignments as a machine gunner!

Drugged Lunch

It was obvious that the platoon was racially divided, even though we were fighting the same war. In the Mess Hall, where we ate our meals, the black and white soldiers sat at different tables. It was no secret that the soldiers who went out first in the field to fight the Vietcong and North Vietnamese troops were black.

One afternoon, I walked in to get a bite to eat. I grabbed a tray, filled it with food and walked to the newcomer's table. It was obvious that the soldier sitting across from me had a drug problem. His speech was slurred, and he would stop talking in the middle of a sentence.

He intermittently woke to put a fork full of food in his mouth only to take a few chews then fall back asleep. As saliva and chewed food oozed down and out the corner of his mouth, his head bobbed up and down above his tray.

Eventually his face lowered all the way into the food, then he was motionless. I thought he would suffocate so I called out to him for a response, but he didn't answer. A senior soldier then came over to the table, checked his pulse, and said emotionless that he was dead.

Even though several people witnessed his death, it did not stop them from using any drugs. Everyone in my platoon made a death pact. I knew that I did not want to live if I was seriously wounded.

Those that were wounded may have returned home, but they were already dead within. To return home with no limbs and having someone take care of you for the rest of your life is unbearable.

People that have spent no time in a war would not understand the death pact, but we wanted our independence more than life. We came to terms within ourselves that if asked we would honor our fellow soldiers' wish to help end his suffering while in combat.

Looking back at that decision now, it is almost inconceivable that I agreed to this pact. We were in our early twenties, and we saw the world through an undeveloped and immature mind.

Infantry soldiers were pulled into the fields, while the duty to guard the outpost and base camps were left up to non-infantry soldiers.

I sometimes guarded the perimeter but a lot of the other dangerous assignments I was forced to do will never be said out loud. These things were so detrimental, but they needed to be done for our survival.

I am not proud of those moments but for us to survive, we all had to do what we had to do. In every situation I was always on high alert because I was afraid of getting killed by Viet Cong.

Being exposed every day to death and destruction, was making me more and more callous to the pain of the injuries of other soldiers, and to the Viet Cong. I was slowly turning into an emotionless human being; I was becoming a killing machine.

We were told that the Viet Cong were uneducated peasants, but that was not true. During the night, they utilized the knowledge gained by working on the compound to inflict damage on many soldiers.

The Vietcong soldiers knew they were not able to stand toe-to-toe with heavily armed and well-trained American soldiers, so they used psychology against us. When we spent long hot hours on search and destroy missions, the Viet Cong made booby-trapped rest areas full of hand grenades, pits with bamboo spikes, and concealed swinging logs suspended from trees. This always kept us on edge, never able to fully let our guard down. There were many attempts to always ambush us.

Even though I lived in one of the worst inner cities in the United States, growing up I was not exposed to a lot of things that I was experiencing in Vietnam.

In Vietnam, soldiers had a choice of how to survive this hell hole, mentally, either you ingested drugs or drank alcohol. For the soldiers stationed in Southern Vietnam they were not exposed to the constant fear of dying, but since I was in North Vietnam, the worse place to be, I chose alcohol. Alcohol helped me to numb emotional pain and to temporarily retreat mentally.

Split Second

I recall an incident where my guilt still haunts me to this day. On one assignment, I was ordered to man a fifty-caliber machine gun, mounted on a truck's cab.

Troops at a neighboring outpost needed supplies bad, so we had to deliver them. I felt so vulnerable and exposed being on top of the truck cab as we highballed through the villages to the outpost. The locals scurried from the street clenching their baskets against their chest running to their huts as our convoy barreled through at high speeds.

As I stood in the open truck with my hands firmly locked around the machine gun, I envisioned the Viet Cong's bullet piercing the back of my head severing all motor functions in my spine. I shook the treacherous thought out of mind because I had to stay focused on the mission before us.

I soon noticed a commotion occurring in the street ahead by the locals causing our convoy to stop. This is it, I thought, a staged attack. As images of my mother, sisters, and brothers ran through my head, my heartbeat pounded forcibly against the wall of my chest.

My eyes scanned the area, looking for any sudden movement as I rested my trigger finger on the gun lever. Suddenly, a little boy no older than I was when I played in fields building my first tree house, pushed his way through the crowd with his arm cocked in a throwing motion.

I turned the machine gun quickly around and pointed it at him. Everything seemed to happen in slow motion. What does he have? Pull the trigger! It's a small object. Pull the trigger! Is it a hand grenade? Pull the trigger! What if it's not?

Pull the trigger! No one would blame me if I did.

Pull the trigger echoed louder and louder, as my mind raced with beads of sweat drizzling down from my temples. The boy and I locked eyes, as my finger began tightening on the trigger. Within a split second I had a decision to make. A grenade? A bag of candy? Pull the trigger?

Like I said at the beginning of this chapter, some things done in Vietnam are better left unsaid. Let the ghosts remain on that land.

Mine Reversal

I had been in Vietnam for at least seven months at this point and the weather was always eerily misty and raining. Several of us had to pull guard duty one evening so we loaded into a truck to be taken to the perimeter.

Once we reached our destination, we collected our weapons and supplies and began walking to our stations. I was ordered to pull guard duty from a bunker, not in one of the foxholes partially filled with water. The other soldiers used their hands and whatever material laying around to dip water from those foxholes before they crawled in.

The Viet Cong knew this would be a good night to strike because of the weather and that we were always in a vulnerable state. We went about our nightly duty of setting mine traps, to face toward the enemy's direction of any anticipated approach. I was responsible for manning the firing mechanism of the mines.

When it became pitch dark, we heard the rustling of the tall grass blades and the clacking of metal against metal on the outside of the perimeter. Darkness can play mind games.

We set off a few flares only to see Viet Cong bodies moving quickly through the grass retreating as they spoke in their native language. I had the mine firing mechanism in my hand ready to fire, but at the last minute a small, still voice told me not to.

The next morning when we went out to investigate the wire, we discovered that the Viet Cong had infiltrated the barbwire and turned the mines to face us instead.

If I had pressed the activation button to the mines, it would have caused major injury or death to all of us guarding the perimeter. Fighting back tears, I sat and wrote this poem to reflect how it felt to be so far from home with the weight of other soldiers' lives in my hands.

Thanks For Giving

Even though I will not be able
to spend Thanksgiving at home this year,
I want to say, Thanks mom for giving me life!
Thanks, mom, for giving me the strength to be alone,
Thanks for giving me the wisdom to know right from wrong,
Especially now when I'm so far from home,
But most of all, thank you mom
With you in my heart, I will never be alone

Black Milk

Race relations were bad in Vietnam. The further north I went in Vietnam, the more I noticed black soldiers being sent to do most of the fighting.

My platoon got a base camp relaxation pass for the weekend. The first thing we wanted to do was eat a hot meal; afterwards take a long, hot shower and then drink a few cold beers. We rapidly walked to the mess hall to eat.

It was there that I noticed how segregated we were. The black soldiers sat and ate with other black soldiers, and the white soldiers sat and ate with the other white soldiers. The soldier ahead of me in line was black and wore many black power necklaces and wristbands.

As a joke he asked for black milk instead of chocolate milk to the serving staff. He noticed me behind him, so he turned and held out one hand to give "Dap," a black handshake.

I shook my head no and explained that I recently returned from the field, I was tired, and just wanted to get something to eat. He turned back around and walked down the food line belittling every white soldier he encountered.

I got the rest of my food without issuing any tirade against the white soldiers and sat at the table with my platoon. The soldier I encountered in line stood over me demanding that I perform "The Dap" with him. He now had an audience watching our every move, and to make matters worse, he was high on drugs. He demanded again that I do "The Dap" with him in a threatening manner. I then stood up and said,

"Let us be! I am here with my platoon for the weekend, and we just want to be left alone!"

It must have been the way I said it or the expression on my face because the soldier backed down and didn't mess with me or my platoon ever again. The look in my fiery eyes showed that I was ready to fight to the death.

I could not wait until we were able to be taken back into the bush, it was my home! I am out of my comfort zone! I am a tunnel rat, I belong underground!

I wear the name like a badge of honor. Like a mole, I do not need my sight underground because underground is where I am king! All I need is my sense of smell and my keen sense of hearing. With both senses, I find my target easily.

I have been chiseled and honed into a precision killing machine. Point me in the direction of my target and I will eradicate him. When a target is close to death; I never look into his eyes because if you did his soul becomes yours.

Souls Intertwined

I remember the day that my soul became intertwined with another. With no tunnels in sight, I had to walk on the surface during our patrol. As we walked through the swaying dark-green, tall elephant grass, with my trigger finger clenched and ready on my M16, the breeze seemed to beckon for us to find its hidden treasure…Viet Cong.

With every light step through the grass my heart pounded in my ear canal causing a hard thump against my chest.

I hoped no one could see the sheer terror and panic in my eyes and how frightened I was. We were trained not to show our emotions and to feel no fear. But how could you not when you are face to face of impending death with every step you take in the unknown.

This was my first time on daytime patrol and all I could think about was how much hand-to-hand combat training I had forgotten because I was accustomed to the dark.

I fought underground with my senses with no sight in the tunnels. I was king in the tunnel world; they were of no match to me. Once the kill was over, I never saw their faces just darkness.

As my squad walked through the thickly laced elephant grass looking for Viet Cong, I became paralyzed with fright, imagining a Viet Cong leaping from the protection of the grass and thrusting a bayonet through my heart, worse yet, I feared stepping on a land mine and blowing myself to pieces.

I longed to be back underground, which was the only place I felt in control and safe. By letting my mind wander, I lost sight of my platoon. Which way did they go? I am now separated and scared. I can't call out for fear the Viet Cong would hear me, and I can't run because of the booby traps.

I turned around three times gun still cocked and hand on trigger, but I didn't know which way they went, so I was left with no choice but to pick a path. I began walking slowly and as quietly as I could through the grass. My heart was racing and pounding so violently that I could feel its pressure in my throat thinking it would choke me to death. My breathing was uncontrollable, I was sure it was my time to die.

My eyes gazed at a still small object in the grass up ahead. Is it my platoon? Did they find me? Had they come back to rescue me? No! It was VIETCONG!

Before I could think about what to do, he leaped from the grass and jumped on me so fast I thought he had been propelled by springs. Things were happening so fast that I didn't realize he had no weapon. He grabbed my fatigue jacket faster than I could point and fire my M16 in his direction.

He wrapped his arms around my body in a death grip and squeezed. The thoughts in my head were in every direction, I was so scared. I closed my eyes, stopped breathing, and waited for the other Viet Cong to leap from the grass to thrust their bayonets in my body. I wanted it over fast, I did not want to suffer so I dropped my weapon to succumb to my fate.

The Viet Cong's face was inches from mine, his hot breath smelled as if he had eaten rotten cabbage which caused my eyes to water. I stared into his eyes as he stared back without blinking. When I realized no other Viet Cong soldier was jumping from the grass; that it was just the both of us, my underground senses kicked in.

Suddenly, my fear was replaced by a rush of adrenaline that filled my body from head to toe. I was ready and looking forward to the combat. The only weapons I had and needed to defend myself were my head and my hands. The Viet Cong still had me in a bear hug.

After realizing he was shorter than me, I head butted him in the nose with all the strength my neck muscle and God would give me. The force of the hit caused the Viet Cong to release his bear hug and to grab his nose.

Bright red blood squirted through his fingers as he became frightened by the amount of blood gushing full force like water from a faucet. For a split second, I felt remorse for what I had done, but then I snapped back to reality and realized I was in a battle for my life.

If one of us had to die, it was going to be him! I was surprised by the amount of damage my head butt had caused as I looked down at my blood covered fatigue jacket. His nose was split open exposing the tissue underneath, and a large gash swelled over his right eye which was beginning to bleed profusely.

I now had the upper hand as I grabbed him in my own bear hug. Tears ran down my cheeks as I wrestled him to the ground. I didn't know if the tears flowing from my eyes were from the adrenaline rush or knowing one of us was going to die. He twisted and turned trying to get out of my grip, but I tightened my arms even more. Should I let him escape?

Should I let him live? That's not a question I struggled to answer, this kill is for me and my platoon's safety. I wanted him to lie, but deep down I did not truly want to take his life.

As I climbed on top of him and pinned his arms to his side with my legs, I laced both thumbs together, grabbed him around his neck and started to squeeze. My special training as a tunnel rat had come back to me. We were taught how to kill with the only weapon able to get through the underground caves, our hands.

The harder I squeezed, the louder I subconsciously yelled like a lion that captured its prey and drowning out its call for help. His hands broke loose and desperately clawed at my laced thumbs around his neck trying to loosen my death grip. I could feel his boney fingers dig into my flesh which caused my hands to bleed. My blood ran down his neck as my grip grew stronger. His grip grew weaker as he gasped for air. My tears began to drip on his face as I stared into his pleading eyes begging for life.

Like a baby falling asleep in their mother's arms, I felt the moment his life left his body. His eyes and mouth remained opened as his arms flopped down on the greenery. In the tunnels, taking a life was easy because I did not see their eyes! Eyes are the windows to a person's soul. I released my grip from his neck and an uncontrollable shout as I stood and stared down at my prey, my fallen opponent.

A hand touched me on my shoulder which released another wave of adrenaline. It had to be another Viet Cong! I jumped up turned to face a foe, ready to take another soul.

"Louis…Louis… snap out of it, what the hell happened to you?" asked one of the soldiers as he quickly stepped backwards.

They stood frozen and shocked at the amount of blood on my face and hands. I was in a state of shock, as I stood over the lifeless body.

"Louis! Louis!"

Everyone continued to yell as they tried to snap be back to reality.

> "Hey, you got your first Gook! Don't worry, the next one will be a lot easier."

They didn't realize that this wasn't technically my first kill, but it was my first above ground. The other soldiers shook my hand and patted me on the back as we began our walk back to base camp. I was emotionally and physically drained, still dazed.

As we entered the base camp, my squad continued to celebrate and told others about my conquest. Like a zombie, I walked to my hooch and collapsed on my bunk. I was now able to think about what had just happened because the adrenaline rush subsided.

I still see the look of fear in his eyes as his life's light slowly diminished. His eyes are burned into my soul forever; he is now a part of me. It's haunting to know that you are the reason why someone did not take their next breath.

I remained laying on my bunk with my eyes closed, afraid to get up, fearing I would wake up from this dream and be back standing over the Viet Cong's body.

So many thoughts ran in my head. It was now over a year since I left the United States. I wondered if my mother would recognize me when she saw me again, but I was worried that I loved the smell of napalm too much.

I was not ready to leave my hooch yet and be exposed to the other troops. Thinking about my mother and being home really brought me down. Finally opening my eyes, I looked at my fatigue jacket. It still had dried blood that turned a deep dark black color. I turned to the other side on my bunk bed and tried to go back to sleep to forget.

I'm not sure which was worse, walking above ground in the tall elephant grass or crawling through the dark tunnels. I went to Vietnam to be a computer operator instead I became proficient with a sixty-caliber machine gun.

Because of my small stature, I was told to go into tunnels to see whether there was information in it that could be of any use to us. I always carried only a knife, nothing else. Many times, it wasn't long before I came across a Vietcong soldier deep in a tunnel.

Here again it was either me or him in a fight for life. We tussled and knocked each other up against the dirt walls. Once again, I relied on my other senses beside sight, therefore their soul was not seen.

A Hasty Departure

After being in the country for so long; always afraid of dying and not having a place to let your guard down, I became cold hearted and callous. I was no longer afraid of dying or causing anyone else to die. I began looking forward to the adrenaline rush from fighting in a hostile situation, so I was no longer afraid of avoiding confrontations.

My platoon was trained to attack; we lived like wild animals in the field for extended periods of time and we loved it. The military had accomplished its mission of turning us into true killing machines.

There were no evacuation procedures to leave Vietnam, when our time was up then our time was up. I assumed we would be alerted when the time came, however we weren't.

Lying on my bunk early one morning, I heard a lot of commotion outside. At first, I did not want to investigate what was going on, but I did. When I looked out my door, I noticed all the trucks were speeding toward the exit gate of the camp. I had been left!

Once again, I found myself running as fast as my feet would carry me to jump on the back of a truck. I reached out my hand as a fellow soldier pulled me up. Once I got on the truck, I turned to look at what I was leaving behind, and that's when my heart sank, and water filled my eyes.

The children. There were so many little children running behind the truck too. Arms out reached as the tears poured heavily from the faces.

I knew what their fate would be without us being there to protect them. The dust from the truck as it barreled out of the village at top speed, hid the small figures and soon they were out of sight. Even though I was extremely happy because we were heading home, I also felt extreme guilt leaving. The cries of the children have haunted me for all these years.

After living like animals for a year, we were finally heading back to our country. During out-processing, I noticed some platoons were being evaluated separately from other soldiers. The soldiers who were not infantry were sent to a separate location. That's because we could not relate, nor did we know how to interact with regular soldiers. How could we? We spent our days hunting, being hunted, and always on high alert.

The physical exam was over faster than I could strip and clean my M60 machine gun. So, when the doctor finished his exam he gave me a clean bill of health, but I disagreed.

"Doc, I don't know what is going on with my brain, but I know something is wrong. I can feel it, my head feels like it is full of cotton."

As I was trying to explain the rest of my symptoms, the doctor interrupted me,

"Once you get out of country and get reacquainted with your family, everything will be alright."

He closed my medical record and walked out the exam room. He wasn't trying to listen to anything I was saying. I sat there in disbelief and silent. Afterwards, we waited in an auditorium for our names to be called so that we could get our plane ticket.

As I waited, in my mind I replayed what to do if an explosion occurred. I immediately looked around for the exit doors, and for windows. I began believing that we were sitting ducks waiting for the Viet Cong to strike us at any moment. I couldn't relax, my brain wouldn't shut off; I was uneasy being out in the open and not below ground.

After getting my plane ticket, I walked in a large group with the Military Police as they escorted us on the plane. It seemed like hours sitting and waiting on the plane for it to take off. There was silence onboard, we were praying that the Viet Cong wouldn't send a mortar to blow us up before ascending into the air.

We all stopped breathing as the plane lifted off the runway and almost simultaneously, everyone let out a jubilant cheer as we jumped in our seats giving each other high fives. We made it! We survived Vietnam! Or so we thought. I did not realize how the things I did in Vietnam would haunt me for the rest of my life.

When we finally landed at our destination, we were escorted to another out-processing center by the police. As we were walking a group of people gathered behind police barricades yelled and shouted,

"Baby killers! Baby killers! Baby killers!"

There were so many posters and angry people shouting obscenities at us that it became so overwhelming. I thought they would break down the barricades and charge toward us. Spit was hurled at us as they raised their fists ready to strike.

I tried to rationalize their reasoning for causing this commotion. Did they not realize that we had no choice! Did they not care that a lot of young soldiers did not return to the United States alive.

The protestors had no right to call us baby killers or to spit in our face. Did they have any idea what this was doing to us? They didn't realize that we were under a lot of pressure. We faced death every second and every minute of the day, to kill or be killed.

This time the processing time was even shorter as before. When the doctor gave me my physical, I informed him also that something was wrong with me, and I wanted at a minimum to have it documented in my medical records.

The doctor did not agree. He refused to document my request, so a standoff occurred.

I would not sign the required-out processing form since he did not sign my medical records. I thought the military would concede, so I decided to make a stand and wait them out. I was completely wrong; the military was willing to wait. Under much pressure and distress, I eventually consented to sign the form.

As we waited in the lobby, we watched all the negative press concerning the war. A few of the soldiers who were being discharged decided to make a final stand by refusing the medals that were being awarded due to the participation in Vietnam and to not wear the uniform home. I was one of those soldiers. I did not want to remember.

Once released, I flagged for a taxi and went through the airport looking as if I had never been in the military dressed in civilian clothes. I boarded my plane, flew home, and never looked back. Little did I know that the ghosts came back with me.

Lessons That I Learned

VIETNAM WAS HELL ON EARTH!

Chapter Six

BACK HOME

Different

After being released and pulled from the front lines then flying home, I felt that my job was incomplete. I went to Vietnam as a 112 lb. computer operator and returned home as a 165 lb. M-60 machine gunner and killer.

What am I going to do with those skills?

The government told all returning soldiers who experienced physical and mental problems caused by the Vietnam War would be taken care of. Right? I was so wrong to believe that.

Fitting Back In

I tried to become as neutral as possible flying home on the plane from California. My silent protest was not wearing my uniform on the plane and refusing the Vietnam combat ribbons I earned. I so desperately wanted the last year of my life to disappear from my mind.

After I boarded the plane and took my seat, I tried to sleep during the flight back home, but I couldn't. Once the plane landed, I hastily got off and walked to the baggage claim to get my duffel bag. I did not like being around a lot of people, I felt overwhelmed and out of place.

Everyone was staring at me, or so it seemed. Once they saw the green duffel bag on my shoulder, I read everyone's expressions as I passed them.

Some wondered if I was on drugs, some wondered what I had done, and some wondered if I was safe to be around. I knew the look. I stood on the curb to flag a cab down. A cab soon pulled up close to the curb,

"Welcome home brotha!"

The cab driver was so excited to see me as he hopped out, opened the trunk, and threw my duffel bag inside with a big smile.

He stuck his hand out to shake mine, but I hesitated. I had a flashback of the day when protestors were at the airport standing behind the barriers calling us baby killers and spitting on us. I did not know how to respond. Was this some sort of trick to grab my hand and try to take me down? I reluctantly did a 2-second shake, put my hand down and quickly climbed into the back seat of his cab.

As I rode on the highway, I was extremely nervous. I was not in control; in Vietnam I was always in control. I am above ground, with nowhere to hide. The cab driver tried to start a conversation with me, but I remained silent. I did not know how to make small talk, how could I? I spent the last few years of my life in a tunnel.

"Tell me which one of these exits is yours."

"The next one."

I pointed to the next exit ahead and turned to look back out of the window. I tried to remain as calm as possible until the taxicab reached my neighborhood. It felt as if the cab driver was driving exceedingly slow down the road as if saying to the neighborhood, your son has returned from Vietnam! Come look!

We passed through my neighborhood, everything looked the same, nothing had changed... except for me. As the taxi pulled up to my house, I hesitated to get out.

What am I doing here? I don't want to be here. Take me back to the jungles of Vietnam where I was in complete control, the master of my fate! I no longer know above ground, only darkness and the smell of napalm and burning feces.

The cab driver jumped out and yanked my duffle bag from his trunk. As I got out, I reached in my pocket to pay him for the ride.

> *"Welcome home again my brotha!"*

Were all the departing words the cab driver said as he refused to accept my tip, he then just drove off.

The front door busted open as my family rushed out to see me. I dragged my duffle bag into the house and began distributing a few gifts which I picked up at the airport. But after a moment, the newness of me being home wore off and life attempted to return to normal.

I became lost over time, and I slipped into a deep depression. I did not know who to talk to or where to get help. So much for the military taking care of me when I returned home.

Like I said before, soldiers had two choices when returning to society: drug or alcohol use. I chose to continue using alcohol because in my mind society accepts alcoholics faster than a drug addict.

Life went from experiencing life and death situations every second of the day where I've held grown men throats and lives in the palm of my hand to being integrated back in society. Did they think I would have no problems? Was I to pretend that I'm okay, to act like nothing happened to me for the past year.

The same bar I grew up watching others go to, is now the bar I frequented. As I sat at the bar with my best friend, Ed, I looked around at the other regulars. I saw Sidewinder still dancing for drinks, but he moved a little slower.

What am I doing here, I wondered as I turned around to finish a pitcher of the clubs special, Vodka and lemonade with my friend Ed. I fell into the same daily routine of drinking and hanging out with a few of my friends who did not go into the service. I was spiraling out of control and alcohol was my way of drowning the memories of Vietnam of what I had seen, what I had done.

I was on a self-imposed death wish because I survived the war when other soldiers did not. I promised many of them that I would make sure they returned home, but I could not keep my promise.

Three months after I returned home, I still did not know how to fit back into society. I began drinking heavily and I was completely out of control. I had a good friend call me one evening because he too was struggling being home.

It was ironic to offer words of encouragement and tell him everything was going to be okay when I was experiencing the same emotions. I did not know that would be the last time I heard from him. He committed suicide later that evening.

I bought myself a muscle car, so one day my friends and I decided to go to a lake to drink. Once we arrived, I parked twenty feet away.

"Man this car is sweet Louis!"

We all got out and I began walking towards the lake in the middle of the night as if in a trance. Immediately, Ed realized what I was planning to do, he walked feverishly over to me.

"Hey Louis…what are you thinking?"

Ed kept walking behind me, but I did not respond, my eyes fixated on the goal ahead which was the lake. Ed bear hugged me from behind and we began tossing each other left and right.

"No Louis! I'm not about to let you do this!"

Little did Ed know that the week prior I had gone to a hardware store and bought all the materials needed for a carbon monoxide poisoning. Was I truly going to inhale? Yes. Was I truly going to jump in? Yes. Was I crying out for help? Yes. I didn't know what to do, I was lost and had no one to turn to.

After regaining my composure and listening to my friend Ed, we all got in the car to drive back to the neighborhood. While they made small talk, I was making other plans in my mind. Once I got on the main road, I drifted back off again. I was angry with my life. I put the car in reverse and began driving backwards as fast as I could go.

"STOOOOOOP! STOOOOOOP!"

Everyone was shouting and screaming, then I snapped back to reality and saw how terrified they were. I slammed on breaks as a cloud of heavy white smoke filtered in the air from the tires screeching on the pavement, and everyone jumped out except for my best friend Ed.

"I'll never get back in the car with you Louis, what the fuck are you thinking?"

The others got out of the car and began walking down the road, but Ed was the only one that stayed. He was a good friend of mine that I could always depend on. He always tried to guide me to do the right thing throughout life. My other friend Apple Jack was the opposite. He was always pushing me to do the opposite.

Apple Jack, Ed, and I have been together since childhood. Like many boys who grew up in the 50's, we experienced many traumatic experiences during our childhood. If we had given up on life, no one would have blamed us.

If we had resorted to a life of crime, no one would have cared. Occasionally, I tripped and fell, but Apple Jack and Ed were always there to help me pick myself up. The emotional childhood scars were dug even deeper in my soul after Vietnam.

Two years passed and I was still living the fast life with a daily routine of sitting in the local bar and ordering a pitcher of Vodka and lemonade. One day the bartender made a comment that has stuck with me to this day:

"Aint' it too early to be drinkin' this stuff?" sat the glass down in front of me and walked away.

I was perplexed, those words hit me like a ton of bricks. I began to look around the bar and saw that I was becoming one of the drunks sitting in the bar each day.

"Hey Sadie, I don't think I'll be drinking these anymore."

I slid off the bar stool and stumbled home. That was the last time I ever entered the club to drink. The Vietnam War and its aftermath affected me physically and mentally.

I had nothing to offer to those who offered the slightest shred of compassion. I was a shell and hid my pain in silence, carrying my war time guilt and shame like a weighted chain around my neck, trying to pretend that what I experienced never happened.

When I returned home, I tried to wash away my guilt, my emotional scars, and wounds with alcohol. In the process, I hurt so many people who loved and needed me.

After years of soul searching and receiving help from counselors, I finally was able to come to terms with all the soldiers left in my care that I could not save. I can accept the fact that I was a young man, that was still a kid, but I was forced in life and death situations; either to kill or to be killed.

Therapy

I finally made an appointment to see a VA therapist. Years had passed, I was still lost, confused, angry, and full of guilt. I was sent home from Vietnam to reconnect to an unfamiliar world. No one wanted to talk about the times I tried to end my life, not even me; nor about any of my medical issues. Something was wrong with me, but no one wanted to believe me.

My appointment was for the next day with a counselor; I couldn't wait to talk. The next day, I left home for my appointment an hour early, because I did not want anything to interfere with my meeting with the counselor.

Once I arrived, I eagerly took the elevator up to the fourth floor and went through the door. It was so quiet and clean; magazines laid neatly on the table and the receptionist smiled as I walked up to the desk.

"Hello, my name is Joe Louis and I have an appointment at 10 o'clock."

"Hello Mr. Louis, please take a seat, Ms. Hall will be with you shortly."

Maybe it was destiny that Ms. Hall was assigned as my counselor because her area of specialization was veterans suffering from Post-Traumatic Stress Disorders and other postwar psychological problems.

The receptionist opened the waiting room door and beckoned me to follow her.

"Mr. Louis come follow me, please have a seat, Ms. Hall will be in shortly."

I sat in the uncomfortable leather chair and started to sweat as I waited for Ms. Hall. She then walked in, grabbed the folder on her desk and sat down.

"Hello Mr. Louis, give me one second."

Ms. Hall looked young for her age, she had a small petite frame with long curly brown hair cascading over her shoulders and had Mediterranean skin complexion.

"Hey Doc, what are you writing?"

I was trying to make small talk but all she did was smile and continued to write. So, with nothing else to do until she finished, I looked around her office to determine what type of person she was.

This must be a pet person as my eyes scanned the office surroundings full of animal pictures strategically placed. No personal pictures were on her desk or walls. Maybe this was her way to keep crazy people from learning about her personal life. The counselor finally stopped writing and looked up.

"Hello again Mr. Louis, my name is Ms. Hall, I am your assigned counselor. Do you remember talking to me when you were in the hospital?"

"No, I do not remember too much of anything that happened when I was in the hospital. I hope I did not say anything that would get me in trouble, did I?"

"No you did not."

Immediately the smile vanished from her face.

"Is it okay to call you Louis?"

"Yea, it's okay."

"Mr. Louis, I hope you feel comfortable talking to me because we will talk about things which may make you feel uncomfortable. In the past a few of my clients did not like talking to a female counselor. If you are uncomfortable, I can assign you to work with a male counselor."

Not wanting to hurt her self-esteem, I declined, even though I was a little apprehensive talking to a person who was also so young.

"I'm fine."

"Good, let's get started. First, I need to ask a few basic questions. How many hours a night do you sleep?"

"I sleep at least 2 no more than 3."

"How is your appetite?"

"I eat only when I have to."

"Louis, are you nervous, you wring your hands a lot, do you do this often?"

I did not realize that I was even wringing them.

"May I call you Doc?"

"I don't mind, relax Louis, this is not a deposition. You and I will spend quite a bit of time together and I want you to become as comfortable as possible talking to me."

Even though I told her I was okay, I was still like a cat on a hot roof, waiting to leap out of my skin. I was so afraid to talk about what I was feeling, but I knew I needed help.

"Mr. Louis this is a question I ask my clients to get a feel of how they perceive themselves. In five minutes or less, tell me how you ended up in my office today?"

I thought for a minute and then answered,

"I live my life like a chameleon transforming to survive. I grew up in one of the worst inner cities in the United States hungry and poor as a kid. Either I transform mentally or perish physically was my motto.
I faced so many hurdles and every now and then I tripped and fell. But I always got up, brushed myself off and continued I was awed by life and intrigued by death at the same time.
I wondered what people would think of me if they knew the life I truly lived. Like a chameleon I transformed and pretended certain parts of my life never happened.
I'm not ready to tell the world about my life, but I am ready to stop running from the past.
Well Doc, how did I do on time?"

She did not respond. She had an expression on her face which I still cannot put into words, then she finally spoke. I wondered if I offended her with what I just told her, so I began to panic.

"Why did you jump into the lake?"

Her question startled and stunned me. Why would she want to talk about that? I'm just starting counseling and she wants to talk about this first. So much for easing into things.

"The month of April is what caused me to jump in the lake."

"What do you mean Louis?"

"That is when I went to Vietnam. I asked myself how can I enjoy life and enjoy living when so many soldiers who depended on me did not make it back?"

"Louis, have you carried this guilt with you all this time?"

"Doc, please stop using my name so much, it now sounds so formal. This is my self-imposed penance; I carry the guilt because I lived."

I explained my guilt in more detail and before I knew it my time was up,

"I think we have talked enough today; I'm going to prescribe a medication that will help you feel better. Also, I want to see you again in one week… but one more thing, because you have so much pent-up emotions which still need to come out, I want you to start capturing your thoughts on paper.
What you are experiencing is called Survivors Guilt. You believe that you are at fault for returning home with no limbs missing and no other physical deformities and you're questioning yourself on why you survived, and others didn't.
I want you to get a notebook and start writing everything about how you are feeling and what you need to say. Bring the notebook with you during your next office visit."

I shook my head in affirmation, folded the prescription paper in half, and walked to the reception desk to schedule my next appointment. As I stood at the desk waiting for the receptionist to write it down, I looked around the room.

I wondered which patients were nuts and why they were out in public. Maybe they were thinking the same about me as a few of them stared my way. I stood there numb, so many thoughts running through my head.

"Your appointment is next Thursday at 1pm."

"Thank you."

I took the appointment card and headed back to my car. That wasn't so bad, I thought as I drove home.

I shared an apartment with my childhood friend, Apple Jack. As I was driving home, I hoped that he was not there because I wanted to be alone. But Apple Jack seemed to always pop up when he felt something was not right with me. I parked my car, walked inside and there sat Apple Jack.

"Get off my bed Apple Jack!"

"Hey Louis, did the doctor say you were nuts!"

"No, she didn't, she said I had a lot to talk about so Imma see her once a week."

"Is she good looking? What type of drugs she give you? You gonna share?"

"I don't wanna hear your shit today, Apple Jack. Don't you have somewhere to go?

"Nope! I'm gonna stay right here Louis and watch tv."

I wondered why I still was putting up with Apple Jack in my life, he had been nothing but trouble from the day I met him as a kid.

I decided to go fill my prescription, so I jumped into my Mazda and let the tape player play whatever song was on the tape player and drove to the neighborhood drug store.

As I walked to the counter, I began to wonder what effects this medication would have on me.

"May I help you?"

"Yes, I wanna get this filled."

"Okay, give us about 10 minutes."

"No problem."

As I waited for my medication, I remembered that the doctor wanted me to start writing. I walked over to the stationary department and picked up a large spiral notebook to use. Ten minutes had passed.

"Mr. Louis your prescription is ready,"

I paid for my items and drove back to my apartment with the music volume even higher. As I walked into the apartment, I looked around and saw that Apple Jack had left.

I tore the medication description paper from the bag and began reading. I loved learning any and everything I could about the human body and medicine. I wanted so bad to become a doctor, but Vietnam crushed my hopes and dream of pursuing that. The paper read Paxil is used to treat mental depression, common symptoms include drowsiness, dizziness, weakness, and decreased appetite.

I did not want to tell anyone that I was seeing a counselor for fear of being labeled weak, and I didn't want to get my hopes up of getting better only to have it fail me.

Over the next few days, I experienced a wide range of emotions because of the anxiety of bearing my soul to a person I didn't know, releasing feelings that I had not shared even with my own family. Before my next appointment she requested that I drop my writing off for her to read over.

As I sat in the waiting room on my appointment date, I could only remain seated for 5 minutes before getting up to pace the floor anticipating for my name to be called, then the door opened.

"Joe Louis,"

Just as my first visit, Dr. Hall was writing feverishly as I entered her office stopping for a moment to beckon me to sit in the uncomfortable leather chair.

"Good afternoon Mr. Louis, how are you doing?"

Not knowing how to respond and thinking it was a trick question I gave a noncommittal answer.

"I'm okay."

"I don't expect to see any noticeable changes with the medication you started last week for a few weeks."

"Okay,"

"I read what you wrote, and I must admit, I was a little surprised by the topics you wrote about. So, this is the approach I want to take for our sessions. I call this approach the X factor.
You will start with your life's foundation and work your way up to the present time in your writing. However, during our sessions, I want to start with your military service and work backwards. My plan is to meet somewhere in the middle. Louis do you remember talking to me about the battle when you were in the hospital?"

"No, I don't remember anything about the hospital too clearly. I thought I was dreaming."

"No, you weren't dreaming, you talked about how you felt with the Viet Cong's neck in your hands and how the other soldiers were rejoicing like you just killed a deer. What happened the day after the battle?"

I was caught completely off guard; of all the starting points, why would she want me to start there? I don't want to relive that moment! She could tell I was becoming apprehensive and nervous.

"Louis, you must trust me, there are major occurrences in your life that you need to confront in order to heal and this is one of them."

"All my life I've always been the one people leaned and depended on. So, when it's my turn to do that, I don't know how to do it, I don't know how to trust. That's how I survived, not trusting because my life could be taken at any moment."

"I understand but you're here back in the States, not in Vietnam... I'm here to help you with what pains you the most."

"Leaving Vietnam."

"What do you mean, leaving Vietnam?"

"Don't get me wrong, I was ready to come home, but I left behind a lot of little kids that needed me and I can still hear their cries. Their cries haunt me especially at night."

"Why? What happened?"

"I took food and water to a group of orphaned kids in a small village. But when we abruptly had to leave, that left them open to be attacked by the Viet Cong, and I know without a doubt that they were killed after we left. They chased after the truck reaching their little hands out, yelling and crying."

"Mr. Louis that's not your fault. You had no way of bringing those kids back to the States with you, so they had to stay. You did what you could at that time."

"I've been to hell and back Doc! I've seen people blown up, body parts, people being tortured, and some things that I won't even speak from my lips. I have nightmares! The nightmares haunt me... the nightmares...

She cut me off before I could say another word. She saw how tense my body had become and how labored my breathing became.

"Calm down Louis, take a moment, slowly breathe in then out. Stay focused with me Louis we're going to address each of these traumatic experiences. Trust me."

Trust? I trusted NO ONE!

Help

After two years of drinking and hurting the people, I cared for deeply, I finally was receiving help for my mental issues but now it was time to get physical help.

I had to admit to myself that I was not okay; but how could I be? I, like many other soldiers was sent to a country at the age of 19 and thrust into situations where death was a common occurrence.

Sitting in the doctor's examination room a second time; I nervously waited for the results of all the tests I had endured. A myriad of thoughts entered and exited my mind what if it's a serious diagnosis. What if it was something life changing? Probably the drinking I did in the service and the year after my release is going to be the reason, I thought.

My doctor who was running from room to room soon entered mine, and without looking up from my records he stated,

"Mr. Louis you have a condition called sponge kidney."

He then looked up to read my facial reaction. After pausing a few seconds, he continued,

"I want to order a few additional tests."

"What kind of tests?"

"Nothing to worry about,"

"What are you thinking Doc? I know a little about the body and I would like to know what is wrong."

Without missing a beat, the doctor proceeded to describe my ailment.

"You have a condition called Medullar Sponge Kidney which is a developmental abnormality occurring in the medullar pyramids of the kidney. MSK is characterized by cystic dilation of the collecting tubes in one or more renal pyramids of the kidneys.
The etiology is unknown, so I want you to take an ultrasonographic x-ray to determine if there is any presence of calcification. Any questions?"

"Doc, give me the layman's version."

"Well, looking at your last X-ray it wasn't clear, so I want to make sure that the opaque shadow on your kidney is not serious. Are you a heavy drinker?"

"I used to, but I stopped and now I only drink occasionally. When I was in the service, I drank a lot of hard liquor. Do you think that was the cause?"

"It's hard to say, so we won't speculate. There is another procedure, which I'm recommending for you. Reading your charts, I see you spent a year in Vietnam so I want to be sure that your abnormally high blood counts are not the result of anything you were exposed to while you were over there.
The nurse will schedule the tests for you and all the appropriate information will be mailed to you. Do you have any questions?"

"No."

He then walked out of my room and on to the next patient.

I walked like a zombie though the hospital corridors into the fresh air and took a breath as if I was experiencing it for the first time in my life. I needed to clear the conversation I had with the doctor from my mind. I should have been concentrating on my driving, but my thoughts kept replaying my version of the conversation.

All the drinking I did in the past may have caused my kidney condition and my abnormal blood counts may have been caused by my exposure to Agent Orange in Vietnam, even though the government denies it.

Two weeks later, I drove through rush hour traffic back to the hospital. I was anxiously anticipating the results of my test. Finally arriving I parked and navigated my way through the maze of the hallways.

Finding the wing, which performed my test, I signed in and waited for my name to be called. I looked at the other patients sitting in the waiting room and tried to imagine what was wrong with their kidneys.

"Mr. Louis,"

Like a drone, I stood and followed her into a room to wait for the doctor.

"The doctor will be in to see you shortly,"

"Hey, is that a statement you have to learn to become a nurse?"

I was trying to make light of the situation; however, the nurse didn't find humor in my question so without responding, she turned and left the examining room.

The doctor entered the examining room a few minutes later, just as the nurse said he would.

"Hi, I'm doctor Raja, please sit on the examination table while I flip through your chart,"

After a few minutes I nervously asked,

"Well doc, what's the prognosis?"

"Louis, since you are a Vietnam Veteran, there are a couple of conditions I want to eliminate because of your abnormal blood counts. Normally when I see counts this high, I would be informing the patient of the possibility they had terminal cancer. So, I want you to undergo a few more tests today."

How long do I have to wait to get these results back?"

"About two weeks."

After driving home, I settled in for the evening and thought I needed a beer to calm my nerves. Pulling one from the refrigerator, I popped the tab, listened to the fizz, but I thought about the alcohol question the doctor had asked, so I walked over to the sink and poured it down the drain.

The procedure I needed to go through was having dye injected into my bloodstream. I previously had an allergic reaction to this dye, so the doctor wanted to prepare me before having the test again. For two weeks he prescribed medication for me to take to build up my tolerance to the dye.

I had a premonition the night before the procedure that something would go wrong. But I had to undergo this test, so that they could figure out what was wrong with me.

By this time, I was married with kids, so I elected not to tell them about my premonition. I had no choice but to take the test, regardless of the outcome. So, I started to write letters to my family members, just in case I did not survive. I slid each letter into a large envelope along with my last will and testament and put it in a place where I knew my wife would find it.

Here it is, the day of the procedure, three hours of darkness remained before my alarm clock would sound, so I stayed up. After getting dressed, I took the last two remaining pills that I needed to take before the test.

As I sat in my Buick sitting in the driveway, I paused a few moments before turning on the ignition. I looked at my house for the longest minute thinking that I may not see my family again. As I drove myself to the hospital, morbid thoughts of this possibly being my last time driving came into my mind.

Arriving at the hospital, I parked my car in the parking garage and walked briskly inside, navigating through the corridors until I found the elevators. I entered the first set of doors that opened and pushed the fourth-floor button. I signed in at the receptionist desk and had a seat.

"Mr. Louis?"

The nurse escorted me to a room,

"Sir, please put this gown on and someone will be in for you shortly."

I was given three smocks. After much twisting, turning, and flipping the smocks inside and out, I finally got them on.

Beaming with a sense of accomplishment, I sat on the examining room table and waited for my fate to enter the room. After a few moments, an orderly rolled in with a wheelchair.

"Mr. Louis, I am here to take you to the procedure room, please sit in the chair,"

I obeyed and off we went down the corridor. I tried to occupy my mind with menial things. I felt that the people we passed were admiring the three-piece gown I had defeated in battle.

We turned left, right, left and another right until we busted through a door only to be greeted by four medical personnel.

My first thought was, this staff was not enthusiastic to see me, but I also felt that something was not right with this room. Looking around, I felt it was sparse of equipment.

"Mr. Louis, please lie on the table."

"Hey, I hope you know that I'm allergic to this dye, but I've been taking my medication for the last two weeks to prepare for this test."

One staff member shook his head in affirmation as he assisted laying me down. My mind was saying not to go through with this procedure because of the premonition I had. I felt very strongly that I would not make it through this, but I did not listen, so I laid down on my side.

As I laid on my stomach, the medical staff prepared to administer the chemical cocktail into my spine.

"Mr. Louis, we are ready to begin."

I felt a slight prick through my back. Like a snake, the dye slithered down the veins in my legs numbing them as it also went upward and raced towards my brain. I first fought its onslaught but later succumbed to it. And just like that I could no longer talk or move.

I began wondering if the medical team saw my face. Did they see my expressions? Are they monitoring me correctly?

"Hey, something is wrong!"

No one could hear me; it was mind talking.

"Mr. Louis, I am administering the rest of the dye,"

I felt I was going to die on the table, and no one would be aware of it. I mentally prepared for my fate and then felt a rush of calmness overcome my resistance and turned it into acceptance. Is this how it feels to die?

"Mr. Louis can you hear me?"

"Hey! Why are you shouting?"

"Doctor, something is wrong, Mr. Louis is not responding! "

"I'm okay!"

But everyone acted as if they did not hear me.

"He's convulsing doctor!"

"Did anyone attach Mr. Louis to the monitor?"

The doctor was furious, and he shouted at everyone in the room. I started to feel my body floating close to the ceiling and I looked down at the team working on my body.

Am I dead? I wondered. I was observing the medical staff frantically hooking me to wires, tubes, electrodes, and monitors. But I felt so much at peace. I wanted to drift into the peace, I knew it was death. I forced myself to think about my family before I succumbed to my fate.

"Joe how are you watching what is going on with such tranquility? Why are you not saddened by what you see?"

"Because if this is death or the life after, I am thankful my life is over."

I suddenly realized the words responding to me were not that of my own internal thoughts.

"Wait, who are you? Are you the voice and light that has haunted me for the last thirty years?"

The voice did not respond.

"You asked me why I was looking with such tranquility as they are trying to save my life, if you are my guardian light you know how difficult my life has been.
You know how I struggled as a child. You know of my gut-wrenching guilt for surviving the Vietnam War and of my never-ending shame for hurting so many people after I returned home."

"Do you remember when you almost drowned at Virginia Beach?"

"Now I remember...you are the voice I made the promise to if you saved me! What do you want from me now? I have questioned your existence for over thirty years and now you return? Are you here to haunt me? If you are, you are too late!"

"Joe, you must continue with what I asked you to do."

"What do you mean? It doesn't matter, right now I don't think I would be missed if I did not return. I've hurt so many people and where were you when I was struggling as a child?"

"Doctor, Doctor, Mr. Louis is coming around!"

I opened my eyes and spoke a word to the medical team. They stopped all their recovery efforts for a few seconds and stared back.

"Mr. Louis, you suffered a seizure along with convulsing during this procedure so we're going to keep you for observation." Said the doctor, *"call upstairs and get a room prepared for him!"*
Several days passed and after all the prodding, probing, extracting fluids, inserting fluids, I was released. It puzzled the doctor why my body reacted the way it did with the dye.
I returned home to wait for the results of my test. During the two-week waiting period, I had no choice but to return to a regular work life balance.

During my time spent overnight in the hospital, I did an evaluation of my life; looking at every facet and questioning if I should live any part of it over.

After a lot of soul searching, to my surprise, I decided to make peace and was ready to accept my fate. I also decided if the test came back negative, I would do what I promised years ago which was to start writing *The Letter*.

After thirty years from first being told, I finally knew what I had to write about and why. The two-week period was up, and while I sat at my desk at work the doctor called.

"Good afternoon Mr. Louis, the doctor would like to speak to you concerning your test, please hold."

Even though the pause was only for a few seconds, it seemed like an eternity waiting for the doctor to get on the phone. What am I going to do if it's positive? How am I going to tell my family?

"Mr. Louis all your test results came back negative but the chemicals you were exposed to in Vietnam caused the abnormally high readings, so we will schedule yearly tests."

I didn't know what to say or do before I hung the telephone up. I just sat in my chair for a few minutes, thought about nothing, and stared into space. I will start writing what the voice told me to write because I made that promise.

The Letter: The Life of A Vietnam Tunnel Rat will portray my life as I struggled to survive and the lessons I learned along the way.

It will lead up to the incident that changed my life and how I was affected by it afterwards. I began writing.

CHAPTER SEVEN

My Poetic Phase

    The promise I made to the voice to write **The Letter** never left my mind. I struggled in the beginning, but then was able to resort to writing the poetry that reflected how and what I was experiencing.

    The poems have a great amount of pain attached to them, but they must be written, they must be read, and they must be understood. Some of the poems may seem dark and desolate because they were written during a period of my life when the country seemed to have turned their back on us.

    I wrote **I Could Not Save** as an overview of my life. As a child I tried to save the baby bird that fell out the tree and tried to nurture it back to life.

    As a young adult I tried to save the men in my platoon from facing the inevitable death but couldn't. I had made a promise to be the leader of the platoon. It would be a promise that has haunted me for the past 30 years.

I Could Not Save

It's life when it fell from the nest,
Which was warmed by the mother's heat
Enough food for my brothers and sisters to eat
My dog
My aunt who died in pain
My vow to become a doctor
To not let another poor person die again.
The children as they ran from the Viet Cong's bullets
My kidney as I drank my guilt away
Time to tell Dad how much he meant to me
My dad whose heart just could not beat any longer
The moment all siblings stood around mom's bed

Trying to be a little stronger
My mom, who lost her courageous fight against cancer
My brother's and sister's heartaches
As they said goodbye to mom
And me trying to save them.

The words to **The Government's Independence** poem have always bothered me because I really did not feel what I wrote. I wrote this poem to reflect the mood of the country during the Vietnam conflict. I have wanted to eliminate all traces of this poem from my life, but I could not, like any historical event this poem was a part of me.

The Government's Independence

We the people of this government
In order to form a perfect country
Established famine, insured unemployment
And provided financial aid to the wars of the world
We have come to take back the part of this land
That we gave to those who fought and died
People say we cannot do this, but we say we can
Without us, this country would flourish
We cannot allow this, and we cannot give the people what they want
We, but will not stop the wars
The brave men living, and dead have made our cause a little better
Not freedom wise, but financially and we thank you.

Don't Cry My Brother was written during my dark phase in Vietnam. I had enough of soldier's dying day in and day out.

Don't Cry My Brother

The morning sun hidden behind the clouds
The evening moon hidden behind the sneers
The daily mist diminishes with the tears
Of all the cries of sorrow
Felt for one another
I'm sorry my brothers I could not save you
From the knocks of death on your doorstep

I wrote **Life and Death** in a riddle format because I did not want to come out and say I was afraid of dying which became a constant thought you did not share with other soldiers.
      Over the years, I have wanted to revise **Life and Death** to make it easier to read, however, if I did, I would no longer have the emotional feelings I was experiencing when I wrote this.

Life and Death

Living and dying
Are two different states
Living will eventually transcend into death
Living without being
Or the essences that make you want to live
Will help you see life the way it really is
Death will not

After leaving Vietnam I returned home physically whole, but not emotionally or mentally. Everyone expected me to be the same person I was before I went to Vietnam. I tried to act as if nothing had changed but it did, so I wrote **Soul Quest** to describe what I was not able to tell anyone openly.

Soul Quest

Where flowers grow without rain
Where people search, but search in vain
This emotional place
Men's soul do test
To find answers to their quest

The Letter book is the result of years of frustration waiting for a sign to start writing every ten years, I wrote a verse.

The Letter

1970
Pen in hand
Paper blank
Capture my thoughts
So it can become The Letter
1980
Pen in hand
Blank paper
Complex thoughts
Capture them quickly
But will they become The Letter
1990
Pen still in hand
Paper still blank
No thoughts captured
Not even confused ones
Will there ever be The Letter

The love between a mother and her son is undeniable. I always sat and talked to my mom. We had long conversations as a young boy growing up. When she transcended, I missed her deeply. **Mom** is my attempt to put my first puppy love into words.

Mom

Mom why does my stomach ache when she's near?
Why are all my thoughts of her?
Mom when she smiles, why does my heart skip a beat
Do you think my puppy would like her?
Mom, she spoke to me today
I didn't know what to say
And mom, do you think she love me?
How will I know?
I hope my blushing don't let it show.
Mom, she wants to be with me
For all eternity
But mom, I want and wait and see
If she is the right girl for me

I wrote **Is it Too Late** to describe what men need to say during a relationship before it became too late. Men know what words need to be said but we neglect saying them until it's too late. I wrote it as a self-analysis that all men should do before realizing their relationship is in trouble.

Is It Too Late

Is it too late to say, I love you?
Too late to tell you how much you mean to me?
Too late to say my daily thoughts begin and end thinking about you?

Is it too late to say, I love you?
Too late to say, I will always put you first.
Too late to watch a sentimental movie together?
Too late to ask, how was your day?
Too late to say I love you?

Too late for roses?
Too late to call just to hear your voice?
And most of all,
Is it too late to say
I don't want us to end?

A Night's Promise is about the relationship between two young adults. A young girl is willing to give herself to him completely thinking he will do the same. However, his motivation is to take from her what he needs to replenish his soul. And to not feel regret even after he is emotionally and physically satisfied.

A Night's Promise

Will you promise to share your thoughts, hopes and desires with me?
Longer than tonight?
Will you promise to invite me into your mind?
Will you always be open
Will you always be honest
Longer than tonight?

I promise every waking thought will be of you
I promise when I close my eyes
You will be my only thought
I will share your pain
I will cherish your love
I will caress your soul
I am replenished
Heart and soul
For I am guilty
I was nourished by your trust
Just for the night.

One early morning, not able to sleep and channel surfing, I stopped at an old black and white movie. The couple was having a heart-to-heart discussion about their unborn child. The female said to the male, you will never know how it feels to carry life within you.

Life's Beginning

Awaken thy heart!
Beat for me
I, the one who loves you
I, the one who shared love to create you

Awaken thy heart!
Feel my loves warmth, which engulfs you
Awaken thy heart!
Awaken for me

I wrote **Children** to say they are our flowers of tomorrow. Take care of them and they will bring joy and happiness to your life when you need it most. Water them and they will grow; don't water them and they will surely die.

Children

Children are flowers
If not mutilated,
They will flourish and bring joy to all
Children are resilient
With minimum care, they will survive
If no emotional nourishment
They seek it from wherever it can be found
Children are clay
Shape and mold them
Caress and hold them

Waiting to be shaped and molded
If an opportunity arises
For you to make a difference in a child's life
Act as if its life depends on it
It just may

The Lone Wolf

See him in the distance, proud, defiant and bold!
He is the lone wolf, truly a sight to behold!
Like his hunger his emotional needs did grow
But in front of his pack, he could never let it show

He can never let them know
He was searching for a mate
She entered his lair, love was heard
Emotional fulfillment is what occurred

It was not meant for them to be
He turned away from her for all eternity
His heart did ache and oh how he pined
Hoping, wishing, and praying to call her mine

Now again he travels alone
Suppressing his loneliness
Suppressing his need
For he is the wolf
The lone wolf indeed

I wrote **Sisters** to say how important they are because they can function in many capacities in your life. When you show a need, they will always be there.

Sisters

Sisters are surrogate mothers when needed
Who offer nuggets of advice if heeded

Sisters will offer an ear for a secret
Knowing full well she can keep it
Sisters will offer a shoulder to rely on
Sisters will offer the other shoulder to cry on

Sisters will be your prom date
Sisters will cover for you when late
Sisters will be your sounding board
As long as it takes
For you to practice the words for your date
Sisters should not be taken for granted
For they are the surrogate mothers

I was having a hard time going to sleep one evening, so I wrote **Things I Learned As A Little Boy** reflecting how I felt as I was growing up.

Things I Learned As A Little Boy

Boys don't cry
Socks should match
Girls are interesting
All moms and dads did it
Newborns can't eat candy
Sisters are not really girls
Moms can read your mind
Try to wear clean underwear
Laugh out loud, cry in silence
Your parents should love you
Never put cactus in your pocket
Water can save your life or take it
Love and hunger pains are similar

Don't scratch private parts in public
Overall, girls are smarter than boys
Cats were put on this earth by mistake
People eat when they are not hungry
Love each other the way dogs love us
Finish peeing before you zip up your pants
Dogs don't like it if you put ice under their tail
Cats can't float with a rock tied to their stomach
Never look an angry dog in its eyes at his level
Never look down at another boy who is peeing
Water balloons will burst whether you are in a house or not
Mothers say they are not hungry even though they are
An apple does not keep the doctor away
You can't hold your breath longer than your mom can hold a spoon of medicine
If you want to eat a bee to see how it taste, don't eat a live one
Running after girls in grade school is a passed down tradition
Quiet is what we were when the teacher needed a break
All of these are things little boys learn as they grow up

Forever Broken Pieces of Me

My Mother died in 1991 from Leukemia, but she chose to suffer in silence. When Mom could no longer walk out to her backyard to feed the birds, rabbits, and other wildlife, she was ready to go "home."

Mom hated going to the hospital with passion. However, one day, her pain was so excruciating she asked to go. When we arrived at the hospital to see her, we were amazed by her good spirits. I had just begun taking Pre-med classes, so I knew my mom was not getting better, but the son in me wanted her to recover.

After our visit, Mom said it was time for us to go home so we left, except for my oldest sister. As I left her room, it felt that it would be the last time I would see my mother. Later that evening we received a call telling us that Mom had died, and when she died a part of me left with her.

My father died in 1995 from a heart condition. As he got older, he relied more and more on my sisters to take care of him. My sisters were always at the hospital and always by his side, but I was not. I had too much anger from how I was treated as a child, and I couldn't forgive him.

The last time dad was in the hospital, I chose not go to see him. I put doing other activities more important than going to see him. The anger in me kept me from telling him that I forgave him before he died, but I cried at his funeral as any child would cry for losing a parent.

It took years after his death to truly forgive him. I was finally able to accept and understand that he did the best he could do with raising us.

The Letter book led me back home; to heal wounds, mend fences and face emotional firing squads. The war and its aftermath affected me not only physically, emotionally, and mentally; but also, how I interacted with anyone who offered the slightest bit of compassion and love.

It has taken many years of on and off therapy to come to terms with the fact that the first two years after I returned home from Vietnam were more traumatic for me than Vietnam itself.

I felt the guilt of all the soldiers that I could not save and were killed. I felt the pain of all the little kids I had to leave behind. I felt the emotions of a frightened little boy that left home and sent into an unknown world.

When I returned home, I did not realize how deep my guilt was from the war. For the next year and a half, I drowned my guilt with alcohol and in the process, drowned the people who loved and needed me as well. I left loved ones with many emotional scars which may never heal.

The Letter book captures only a portion of my life. There are some subjects that I am still trying to resolve and some I'm not proud of. It is difficult to discuss them in an open forum such as this.

Hopefully, reading *The Letter* book will start the healing process for you. You could possibly understand why I did the things I did when I returned home from hell. It's time for me to finally close this chapter of my life and truly start to live.

Who knows there may be another *The Letter* book in me that's begging to be born.

When I returned from Vietnam, there were many people who I hurt deeply who loved and cared about me. If any of you are reading this book, words cannot describe how badly I feel. I hope you will be able to forgive me even though I know you may never forget.

CHAPTER EIGHT

UNEXPECTED

Ambulance sirens and lights blared on the bumpy St. Louis roads with cars moving to the side making room for it to pass. Finally arriving at the VA Hospital, the ambulance driver jumped out the driver seat and rushed to the back to open the door. He was greeted by hospital staff assisting to lift the stretcher out of the ambulance.

"1-2-3 lift!" one of the paramedics yelled.

"Go to room 3, get the electrodes on him!" shouted a nurse.

Once the stretcher came in the room doctors and nurses came from every direction. The doctor held the EKG print out and peered through his reading glasses.

"You're having a massive heart attack." The doctor said.

"A heart attack...what? You're kidding me." Joe responded in disbelief.

"We have to go to the operating room right now!" the doctor said as he held the EKG print out midair.

Joe rubbed his hand over his forehead shockingly,

"Wait...wait...everything is moving too fast; I'm trying to process this."

"Yes, sir, I know it's fast but there's no time your heart has suffered a lot of damage already." The doctor responded.

"Okay, Doc, what do you need to do?" asked Joe in defeat.

"We have to inject contrasting dye to see where the blockage is located." the doctor said as he peered over his glasses.

"But I'm allergic to that dye." Joe said as he was concerned and hesitant.

"We're going to pump as much medication before giving you the contrasting dye to counter reverse any reactions to it." The doctor said confidently.

"Okay, I'm ready." Joe said as he laid back on the pillows.

The bed was rushed down the hallway with nurses and doctors on both sides. Once inside the operating room, they began passing medical instruments from one side of the bed to the other.

"Let's go people! Let's go! Give him anesthesia and make sure he's hooked up so that we can monitor his heart." The doctor demanded.

"Voice, do you see what's going on?" Hey voice here we are again… voice do you hear me?" Joe telepathically thought.

"I am here… I see what is happening… so what do you think?" the voice.

"My body is worn out, I hurt every day and it's hard for me just to walk to my front door." Joe thought.

"Yes, I know." the voice in agreement.

"I can't do the things I love doing anymore. The last time you told me to go back and write "The Letter" and I did what you asked me to do." Joe thought with sadness.

"Yes, you did." the voice.

"But now I don't want to go back to that body, I'm feeling so much peace." Joe explained.

"Come on people inject that dye... we're losing him... get the paddles... CLEAR!" the doctor yelled.

A soul began to lift higher and higher after each electrical shock.

"Am I going with you this time voice?" Joe asked.

"Yes, you can come if you like, or you can return." the voice peacefully responded.

But this time the contrasting dye had won the battle as the sound of the heartbeat monitor flat lining engulfed the room.

The memories of childhood antics and the faces of family members played continually as a movie reel until a bright white light had complete control followed by peace.

The premonition from 2018 has come true.

Time of Death, 12:20 pm March 26, 2022

Mr. Joe "Louis" Loveless

Afterword

[Phone rings]

I anxiously picked up expecting the doctor to say,

"We've managed to save him, he's in ICU recovering."

I mean why wouldn't the doctor say that? There are so many other people that are living with diseases worse than my father, so why wouldn't he live? But that was not the case.

"Ms. Loveless, we've exhausted all means with your father Mr. Loveless and unfortunately I'm sorry but we could not save him."

"Wait… so what are you saying?" I asked the doctor, "are you saying that he's dead?"

I couldn't hear the doctor's response, my body went numb, my legs went limp, thoughts raced in my mind, and my heart felt tight. It felt like someone punched me in the center of my chest as my world collapsed.

How do you go from talking to someone and them saying, 'Bug, I'm alright…it's okay,' to hearing 30 minutes later someone calling saying they've done all they could do? I was confused. My family and I were already dealing with losing our mother and the circumstances that surrounded her death in 2020, then the death our uncle in 2021, and now the unexpected death of our father in 2022.

I became obsessed with my father's death; he was my rock, my foundation, and my best friend. I ordered his medical records so that I could figure out what happened, even though I knew I could not change the outcome. I read each line of the hospital summary report, but the ending result was that he had a reaction to the contrasting dye. The same dye that almost took his life previously to now having his own death premonition in 2018. All the doctors noted that his case was the most challenging they had ever seen because of all the secondary medical issues that occurred so quickly. I was even more confused; I still had a lot of unanswered questions.

Taking on the daunting task of co-writing his book was not only overwhelming but was also emotionally draining. I relived every childhood adventure, every Western Union letter delivered, and every Vietnam nightmare he dreamt. After co-writing, I then understood that the reason why he never slept in a bed after returning from Vietnam was because once a tunnel rat always a tunnel rat! The confined space of the tunnels, as ironic as their past intended purpose, was his "safe place... his home." And that whatever he was exposed to ultimately caused his death years later on American soil.

He despised having to deliver those Western Union letters to unsuspecting families because of the sadness they represented. But where's my letter at? Where's my letter that says my father's name, the date, and the location he died? At least by receiving that Western Union letter you're not getting your hopes up and then only to tragically be let down. The letter may have been closure for some families to deal with the death of the Vietnam soldier, instead, I received one phone call getting my hopes up high to a second phone call that has forever shattered my world.

That phone call will forever be the substitute of a Western Union letter.

There is no closure,
no hope,
nothing left but unanswered questions.

Printed in Dunstable, United Kingdom